A
DAILY
DOSE
OF
BRAVE

A 30 DAY DEVOTIONAL
Emma Bryant

4

Published in Great Britain in 2023 by Independent Publishing Network

Copyright © 2023 Emma Bryant

ISBN: 978 1 80352 724 6

All rights reserved. No part of this publication may be reproduced, distributed, or transmitted in any form or by any means, including photocopying, recording, or other electronic or mechanical methods, without the prior written permission of the publisher, except in the case of brief quotations embodied in critical reviews and certain other non-commercial uses permitted by copyright law.

Copyright Info can be found, e.g. on Bible Gateway, for example MSG: The Message. Scripture quotations marked MSG are taken from THE MESSAGE, copyright © 1993, 2002, 2018 by Eugene H. Peterson. Used by permission of NavPress. All rights reserved. Represented by Tyndale House Publishers, Inc.

Scripture quotations marked TPT are from The Passion Translation®. Copyright © 2017, 2018, 2020 by Passion & Fire Ministries, Inc. Used by permission. All rights reserved. ThePassionTranslation.com.

Scripture quotations marked (NIV) are taken from the Holy Bible, New International Version®, NIV®. Copyright © 1973, 1978, 1984, 2011 by Biblica, Inc.™ Used by permission of Zondervan. All rights reserved worldwide. www.zondervan.com. The "NIV" and "New International Version" are trademarks registered in the United States Patent and Trademark Office by Biblica, Inc.™

The ESV Global Study Bible®, ESV® Bible Copyright © 2012 by Crossway. All rights reserved.

Scripture quotations marked (NLT) are taken from the Holy Bible, New Living Translation, copyright ©1996, 2004, 2015 by Tyndale House Foundation. Used by permission of Tyndale House Publishers, Carol Stream, Illinois 60188. All rights reserved.

Scripture taken from the Amplified Bible, Copyright © 2015 by The Lockman Foundation. Used by permission.

No one may copyright the NHEB, its versions, or any other file edited by Wayne A. Mitchell. No one may trademark the above noted files. Without changing the text, you may publish, copy, translate, quote, and use the NHEB and versions, and any other file edited by Wayne A.
Mitchell freely without additional permission.

Contemporary English Version: Scripture quotations marked (CEV) are from the Contemporary English Version Copyright © 1991, 1992, 1995 by American Bible Society.

This book is dedicated to Vivienne Hopwood, who taught me to pursue a love for God above all else and really fight for a life worth living. Love you mum x

CONTENTS

HOW TO USE THIS BOOK	PAGE NUMBERS:

INTRODUCTION: 8 - 10
WHAT DOES *'BRAVE'* LOOK LIKE?

PART 1. HOW TO BE BRAVE 11 - 61
DAYS 1 TO 12

PART 2. HOW TO SPEAK BRAVE 62 - 97
DAYS 13 TO 20

PART 3. HOW TO REMAIN 98 - 143
BRAVE
DAYS 21 TO 30

145

ABOUT THE AUTHOR

INTRODUCTION
What Does 'Brave' Look Like?

"Have I not commanded you? Be strong and courageous. Do not be afraid; do not be discouraged, for the Lord your God will be with you wherever you go."
~ Joshua 1:9 (NIV: New International Version) ~

I once heard it said that *'fear is faith in reverse'*.

If faith is *'the substance of things hoped for and the evidence of things not seen,'* as the Bible describes in **Hebrews 11:1**, then fear is the opposite. Fear often has no substance in reality. Often our fears are unfounded, with no evidence to justify our worries and concerns. In other words, most of our fears are about things that we imagine *could happen, might happen*, but actually *never happen*!

Just like a child who imagines what could be lurking in the closet in the dead of night, we can all allow our imagination to create scenarios and images that become a breeding ground for fear. Every time we think about the *'what if'* scenarios we feed the monster called fear, and it grows.

God knew that some of the greatest battles we would face in our lifetime would be those in our mind. He knows what challenges we are facing now and what we will face in the future. He knows how we feel about the circumstances that surround us and how our concerns consume us. Though we do not get to choose the hand that life deals us, we do get to choose our response to it and our response should always be to come to the God who knows us so intimately.

We should be able to come to Him, and say, "but God, you *know* me…".

"Lord, You have examined me and know all about me. You know when I sit down and when I get up. You know my thoughts before I think them. You know where I go and where I lie down. You know everything I do. Lord, even before I say a word, You already know it. You are all around me—in front and in back— and have put Your hand on me."
~ Psalm 139:1-5 (NCV: New Century Version) ~

Even though the trials that you are going through (the problems that trouble you, or the uncertainty you're facing) may have blindsided you, they never blindsided God. He is not only in your life, but also ahead of you in life. Every hurdle you encounter along your journey He has already seen and planned for. They have already been overcome by Him. So we can either focus on the fear of how it all could be, or we can have faith in the one who says, "*trust me*."

The text of **Joshua 1:9** begins with God speaking, "*Have I not commanded you? Be strong and courageous*." Think about that for a moment. Did you know that being brave is a command? He's not *recommending* that we be bold. Neither is he *gently* encouraging us to be brave. He is giving us a direct order.

The word '**command**' means '*to direct authoritatively*' but can also mean to '*dominate (from a strategic position)*' such as a superior height.

It is an order given by someone who has a greater, higher perspective.

When an army is preparing for battle, there is always a strategy, a battle plan. Troops are positioned accordingly and await their orders from the commanding officer who has intelligence on the enemy.

In the Kingdom of God, we must position our lives to be obedient to the commands of God. When an army, in the natural, obeys the commands given to them, there is structure, then there is order, then they get results.

I love how God never left us to figure life out on our own. Instead, He gave us ways to live and commands to follow so that we too might be overcomers: strong and not weak; on top and not underneath; victorious and not defeated.

Life is to be lived. I believe so many precious lives are simply existing, rather than truly living because we have allowed fear to dominate and intimidate us. We have listened to the lie that has whispered that we are less than or inadequate, a failure, or a fake. We have allowed fear to clothe us in the garment of worthlessness and inferiority. We have accepted the enemy's invitation to sit at our table and dine in the company of doubt, disbelief and disappointment.

By far, the greatest lie the enemy feeds you is this: *"You're the only one."* He wants us to believe that no one else thinks like this, feels like this or struggles like you do. Isolation is his weapon of destruction and fear breeds best when you feel alone.

This devotional is written for women from every walk of life, no matter what age or life stage you find yourself at. This is to encourage you and remind you that you are not alone.

You belong to an army of women who face the same challenges and struggles, day in, day out, and this army has a commanding officer who is with you wherever you go. He has already seen your tomorrow before you even go to sleep tonight. He has seen the tactics of the enemy and is aware of the pressures you face.

Father God, for every beautiful warrior woman about to commit this next month to finding new strength in You, I thank you in advance for her. You know her intimately, her needs and fears – You know them all. You know what fuels her and You know what binds her and I pray that You set her free to be all You intended her to be. I thank you for the tears that will flow as she releases her frustration to You, and I thank you for the heart that is healed as You pour Your love into her. She is bold. She is confident and female to the core, and as she opens her mouth, may the Heavenlies hear her roar! Amen.

Now you go, girl!

Emma Bryant

PART ONE

HOW TO

BE BRAVE

DAY ONE
FEAR IS A LIAR

HOW TO BE BRAVE

I am someone who has battled with fear for as long as I can remember. In fact, my earliest childhood memories are not important milestones like starting school or the first time I rode my bike without stabilisers, but rather an emotion that has tracked me for my entire life – a constant feeling of *fear*. Even as a pre-schooler, I can recall the emotionof fear and worry.

Nothing terrible had ever happened to me. But when your emotions take over your imagination, everything gets a little crazy. As I grew older I would make scenarios up in my mind about what could, would or might happen, and fear would grip me.

Fear is like an invisible oversized monster. It turns up uninvited and wants to intimidate you, rule you and ruin you.

But, **fear is a liar** because 'what might be' is not a reality, and 'what could be' has never happened. So don't allow your imagination to feed a fabrication, bringing a fear that feels so real about a circumstance that has not even happened.

> "So do not fear, for I am with you; do not be dismayed, for I am your God. I will strengthen you and help you; I will uphold you with my righteous right hand."
> Isaiah 41:10 NIV
> (New International Version)

When you dwell on the '*what ifs*', you are opening a door in your life for the thief to steal time away from you. You will find hours, days, months and – for some people – years and years of your life wasted, anxiously worrying about something that never was or might never be.

That is time you can never recover, never get back, and time is precious. So let's not allow it to be taken from us through a broken mindset.

Faith is fear in reverse. Think about driving your car. You cannot have it in first gear and reverse at the same time. Both positions have the same power to move the car. But you must choose the direction you want your vehicle to go in. If it's forward, then you can't have it in reverse.

It's the same for your life. Wherever your thoughts go, your life will follow. If you have dreams and aspirations for the future, then you have to focus on going forward. You cannot be full of faith and filled with fear at the same time. **1 John 4:18** teaches us that '*there is no fear in love, but perfect love casts out fear*.' He also says, 'God *is* love' (my emphasis). So God doesn't just have love to give. He actually is **love itself**!

So when your imagination starts running and thoughts of panic or dread come over you, don't just change your thoughts to think about something else. Focus on God: read from his life-giving Word, pray to Him, sing about Him, because His love trumps fear every time.

Life can be tough at times and none of us can predict our tomorrow. Given the chance, the enemy would love to get into your mind, unpick your thoughts and wreak havoc in your imagination. Focusing on God and His Word keeps the door of your imagination shut to the enemy. It energises us, salvages our time and allows us to live and move freely in life.

Life is real. The struggle is real. I have come to realise that fear is very much part of this world and therefore is likely to always be around. ***Fear is an emotion that we feel, but a temporary feeling that we can defeat.***

So remember today to commit your day to God and stay focused on His love and His goodness. Don't allow the enemy to steal any more of your precious time through fear.

PRAYER FOR TODAY
Lord, today I remind myself of the words you spoke in Isaiah 41:10, 'do not fear, for I am with you; do not be dismayed, for I am your God. I will strengthen you and help you; I will uphold you with my righteous right hand.' Amen.

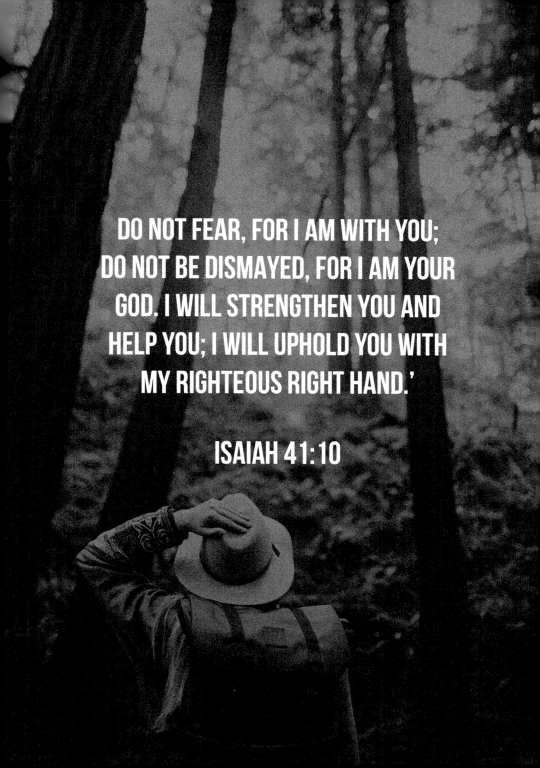

YOU ARE SO INTIMATELY AWARE OF ME, LORD. YOU READ MY HEART LIKE AN OPEN BOOK AND YOU KNOW ALL THE WORDS I'M ABOUT TO SPEAK BEFORE I EVEN START A SENTENCE! YOU KNOW EVERY STEP I WILL TAKE BEFORE MY JOURNEY EVEN BEGINS.

PSALM 139:3-4

DAY TWO
PUNCTUATE BEFORE YOU EXASPERATE

HOW TO BE BRAVE

Every day that you wake up is a brand new gift to you, unopened, unused, a day just waiting for you to discover. It's a part of your story that hasn't happened yet, a page that's waiting to be written. So, before it begins, decide *'how do I want my story to read*?'

What gets recorded in your story today isn't the events that do or do not happen, but rather your response to those events – your attitude, your mindset, your decision-making. Will you allow God to lead you or will you fly through the day, driven by emotion?

Whenever you read a good story in a book, the punctuation can make or break that story.

Punctuation allows you to pace yourself, draw breath and pause for contemplation. Without it, you would read on recklessly, losing the meaning; it would leave you breathless.

It's the punctuation in your life that makes room for the Holy Spirit to edit your story. Maybe you could prayerfully ask God to show you how to do it.

I want you to ask yourself the question, *'what will my response be to whatever life presents*?'

So, today, how will you write your story?

WHERE DO I NEED A COMMA, ALLOWING MYSELF TIME TO BREATHE?

So often we race through our day, meeting deadlines and trying to keep up with busy schedules, and then we fall into bed – exhausted! The past 24 hours seem a blur.

Give yourself permission to pause, rest, hold back, think, ponder, wait. Not everyone needs an answer right now.

Not every message needs an immediate response. Not everything needs your imminent time and attention. Some things can wait. A comma in a sentence is not the end. It's simply a place where you can pause, take a breath, and then go again.

PUT SOME FULL STOPS IN PLACE

Decide at the start of the day, '*it's okay for me to say no*'. Don't put up with what you don't have to. Full stops can be very liberating. Put a full stop to that conversation if it's gossip or idle chit-chat. Don't waste your precious story giving time and attention to it. Put a full stop to your attitude. Don't allow negative emotions – like fear, anger or jealousy – to write themselves into chapters of your life.

It's okay to say, "no". It's okay to say, "enough". It's okay to say, "I'm done with that." It's okay to walk away or say, "not today". It's okay for you to take charge of you and put in a full stop.

EXPECT A FEW EXCLAMATION MARKS!

The unexpected surprise, the thing that doesn't go according to plan, a turn of events that you didn't expect. Every day will give you at least one exclamation mark that you weren't expecting!

But remember, it's not a roadblock. It's more like a hurdle, and the God who goes before you in all things will navigate you. He will help you get over it, past it or around it. Nothing in your life is a surprise to God. He knows your future. He's in your tomorrow. So, though that unexpected thing took the wind out of your sails, it hasn't shocked Him and He's not left wondering what to do about it!

But most of all, at the end of this day, may you reflect and remember that although you thought you were writing this chapter, the pen was always in the hands of the most skilled and ready writer, as He beautifully crafts His desired destiny for you and records your story in His eternal journal. Sometimes the bravest thing you can do is to say, "I surrender my will to your perfect plan. Punctuate my life, Lord."

PRAYER FOR TODAY
God, *I thank you that each day you've gone before me and you know what's ahead of me. You know what will bless me and what will challenge me. Therefore, I trust in you to be my counsel and my guide as each new day unfolds. May I never waste a moment of the precious gift of time that you have given me today.* Amen.

DAY THREE
BE ALL IN

> *"Don't just listen to the Word of Truth and do not respond to it, for that is the essence of self-deception. So always let His word become like poetry written and fulfilled by your life."*
> *James 1:22 (TPT: The Passion Translation)*

HOW TO BE BRAVE

Okay. Time to put your big girl pants on as this is going to require us to be truly honest with ourselves.

We've all heard it said, *'be doers of the word, and not hearers only,'* right? Now take a moment and ask yourself, *'am I truly living my life in the way God's Word is teaching me? Or am I treating God's Word like a pick 'n' mix sweet stand, taking the bits I fancy and leaving what I don't like, according to how I'm feeling?'*

My son plays football and when he was young I used to think I was a good supporting mum. However, the football club thought very differently. They called me a *'seasonal supporter'*. In other words, they knew if the sun was shining Emma would be there, looking the part, cheering on the team. But if the weather changed and the rain clouds gathered, they knew I would be nowhere to be seen.

I thought I was a true supporter. But it was those who braved the weather, who turned up to the match no matter what, who were the committed ones who were *'all in.'*

When it comes to the teachings of God's Word, He asks us to be *'all in'*. Picking and choosing the bits you adhere to and choosing what you leave out only deceives *you* – not God, not your friends – just yourself. We have to remember, all of God's Word is life-giving and good, enabling you to be the best possible version of *you*! When you become selective in it, you end up cheating yourself out of your very best life.

There are parts of the Word of God that make you go, "wow," and parts that make you go "ow!" Some scripture will make you bloom and with others, you'll see areas He wants to prune. There are times He wants to bless you and times He needs to correct you. Sometimes He rests you, other times He stretches you. There are seasons where His Word to you is, "Go," and seasons you'll hear a definitive, "No."

Our scripture today says, *'let His Word become poetry, written and fulfilled by your life.'* What a beautiful concept, that He is the writer and I am here to live out the life that He has already scripted for me. Bravery begins when you decide to live in a way that the scriptures teach, rather than the way the world dictates.

PRAYER FOR TODAY
Lord, I pray that you help me to follow you in every way, that my whole life would become a reflection of you, as I take all of your word and allow it to shape me. Amen.

"LET YOUR LIFE REFLECT THE FAITH YOU HAVE IN GOD. FEAR NOTHING AND PRAY ABOUT EVERYTHING. BE STRONG, TRUST GOD'S WORD, AND TRUST THE PROCESS."

Germany Kent

SO ALWAYS LET HIS WORD BECOME LIKE POETRY WRITTEN AND FULFILLED BY YOUR LIFE

JAMES 1:22 TPT

DAY FOUR
WHAT CAN YOU IMAGINE?

> *"... Nothing they plan to do will be impossible for them."*
> *Genesis 11:6*
> *(NIV: New International Version)*

HOW TO BE BRAVE

This scripture was written about the people of Babel who thought they could reach God by building a tower up towards Heaven.

I mean, think about it. They managed to build this enormous monstrosity of a tower thousands of years ago, with no machinery or technology. All these men with their bare hands, their imagination and sheer willpower!

As you read through the events of this story in Genesis, you will see how God stepped in and put a stop to their ambitious plans. He knew the mind of possibilities within them, for he had created and designed mankind in His image and likeness. He knew that if they could imagine it, then they could have it. Imagination is the ability to bring our creative thoughts to life.

As children, we are told to stop dreaming, be realistic, stop living in a fantasy world, get a real job and grow up! But I want to remind you today that your imagination is a gift from God.

Our limitless God hardwired a creative and imaginative mind within you because He wants you to know a limitless life. He created you to dream, to think big, to experience life outside of what most people call *'the norm.'*

Your imagination was given to you. It sets the course of your life when your life is submitted to God, to take you in the direction He has planned for you.

So here is your permission to think big!

Think outside the box life has put you in. Think past the lids and labels others have put on you and begin to dream the life you want to live. Who knows? Maybe *'nothing you plan to do will be impossible for you!'* But if you never think it, fail to imagine it, can't dream it, you will never know it.

This is your new day. Go for it!

IMAGINATION IS THE ABILITY TO BRING OUR CREATIVE THOUGHTS TO LIFE.

Emma Bryant

Remember, it takes a brave person to think big, because when you do you open yourself up to criticism. But the God of impossibilities made you in His image. So what you can imagine you can do, you will do. Insecurity will always want to keep you small.

So don't let intimidation become your limitation. Go ahead and dream girl!

PRAYER FOR TODAY
Lord, help me to imagine myself in the way that you see me, rather than seeing all my faults and flaws, trying to live up to the expectations that others have put on me. Today, as I submit my thoughts to you, I give you permission to increase and expand my mindset. Help me to imagine what my life could be like under the influence of a limitless God. Amen.

DAY FIVE
I'M MEANT TO BE ME

"You saw who you created me to be, before I became me!
Before I'd ever seen the light of day, the number of days you
planned for me were already recorded in your book."
Psalm 139:16
(TPT: The Passion Translation)

HOW TO BE BRAVE

When God made you, He made three different components to you: your body, your soul and your spirit. Therefore, He's interested in all three elements of you.

So often we find ourselves talking about pursuing our dreams or finding our God-given calling (our reason for being). I wholeheartedly believe that God wants us to pray, seek Him, and find out His plans for our lives. But have you ever considered that God needs your **body** to be healthy, your **spirit** (your conscience and intuition) to be right, your soul (your mind, will and emotions) to be steady and sound, for Him to execute His purpose for your life?

If God created you to live in a body, feeling and knowing emotion, with a spirit that connects with Him, then he is concerned with the health and welfare of **all of you**.

Whether you love your **body** or wish for it to be different in size, shape or colour, whether it has scars or blemishes you try to hide or you have an inability or a disability that frustrates you – it is your body – the only one you have. So learn to love it. Be thankful – so very thankful for it, because without it there wouldn't be an expression of you on the earth. Diligently take care of your body. Consider what you eat! Do you fuel your body with the healthy nutrition it needs, or do you fool yourself into believing that everything that tastes good is good?

Look after what you have, because – here's the deal – while there is breath in your body, there is a purpose to your life and a possibility for you to pursue hidden dreams.

Keep your mind (soul) healthy. How do we do this?

'The number of days you planned for me were already recorded in your book.'

Psalm 139:16

Well, the Bible tells us: *'Fix your thoughts on what is true, honourable, right, pure, lovely and admirable. Think about things that are excellent and praiseworthy.'*

You get to decide what you dwell on or ponder over. We consume information all day, every day, by what we see and what we hear, and this often affects how we feel. Some of the information is helpful and some of it is hurtful. We have to be mindful to filter what we take in and absorb. We need to be wise stewards of our minds and dwell on the helpful, wise, encouraging stuff.

- You don't need to watch every latest Netflix series if it's going to provoke thoughts of fear.

- You don't need to watch every social media feed if it's going to produce emotions of jealousy.

- You don't need to engage in every conversation if it's feeding you gossip - ***you get to choose.***

Lastly, keep your **spirit** healthy. Get planted (fixed, remain, stay) in your local church. Be sure the intake of the Word of God is a daily habit for you. You can do this through music, podcasts, apps, books or simply by picking up your Bible.

I'm a huge fan of accountability. Don't try to be your own counsel, but rather lean in, ask questions and listen to the wisdom from someone older, wiser and further on in their Christian faith than you are.

PRAYER FOR TODAY
Lord, I thank you that I am beautifully and uniquely made by you, on purpose and for a purpose. I ask that when it comes to looking after myself, you give me wisdom where I'm lacking, strength in the areas I feel weak, and an understanding that if I'm not dead then you're not done with me yet! So, I embrace my future with you and ask you to help me to become the best version of me possible. Amen.

FIX YOUR THOUGHTS

on what is true,
honourable, right, pure,
lovely and admirable.
Think about things that are
excellent and praiseworthy

Philippians 4:8 NLT

DAY SIX

ALLOW YOUR PROBLEMS TO PRODUCE PERFECTION

> *"For you know that when your faith is tested, it stirs up power within you to endure all things. And then as your endurance grows even stronger it will release perfection into every part of your being until there is nothing missing and nothing lacking."*
> *James 1:3-4*
> *(TPT: The Passion Translation)*

HOW TO BE BRAVE

It is true that our faith does not grow during the good times. But rather it's in our challenging situations, our difficulties, it's in the curve balls life throws at us that faith is produced. It's like the rose bush that blooms more beautifully the more horse poop it has dumped on it!

Faith is developed when we must trust God in a seemingly impossible situation.

Something that looks as though it will never be solved (and in the natural, it probably never could be) keeps us awake at night. It's a crisis, a problem, a situation that you know needs a miracle and so you are praying and believing for God's almighty intervention with unshakable confidence that He *will* supply all our needs according to His riches in glory.

Scripture tells us that when we are in faith for something, it grows endurance within us. Isn't that fascinating?

If we have **Hope** (that is, *faith*) in God, He in return gives us a coping mechanism in the waiting – **Endurance.**

Endurance is the ability to keep doing something difficult, unpleasant, or painful for a long time. Now, this is where it gets good!

Your endurance *produces* something. Kind of like an olive that produces oil when pressure is applied or a coconut that releases milk when it's broken. In other words, there is something more within you that is not seen until you've been squeezed or broken at some point in your life.

Endurance *"releases perfection into every part of your being"* so that every area of your life – your physical health, mental health, mind and emotions, is affected by it, so *"nothing will be missing and nothing will be lacking"* in you.

Okay, let's pause for a moment and think about that.

When you emerge from your difficulty, having had to endure suffering and uncertainty, you're going to emerge differently. Kind of like a butterfly emerging from a chrysalis.

It went in as a caterpillar and came out as a completely different creature, taking on a new form, with different abilities and a renewed strength, all after having to endure a season of change.

The scripture tells us that **perfection** will come to every part of your being. Perfection means the process of improving something until it's faultless.

- **Perfection in your body:** It means fullness in health; higher energy levels; an increase in strength to your bones and joints; it means every cell, sinew and fibre of your body is aligned, refreshed and restored.

"My son, pay attention to what I say, turn your ear to my words. Do not let them out of your sight, keep them within your heart. For they are life to those who find them and health to one's whole body."
~ Proverbs 4:20-22 (NIV: New International Version) ~

- **Perfection in your soul**: The ability to be at peace on the inside even when life is stressful on the outside; it's the ability to remain faithful and hopeful, even when a situation looks hopeless; it's the ability to exercise self-control so you are not being driven by your feelings, according to your daily circumstances.

"Praise the Lord, my soul; all my inmost being, praise His holy name."
~ Psalm 103:1 (NIV: New International Version) ~

- **Perfection in your spirit**: To be made fully aware that you are in right standing with God; the inner knowing that if He is with you, you cannot fail; you learn to listen to and rely on that quieter, calmer, inner voice to lead you, rather than being strung out by emotions that scream at you.

"For the Spirit God gave us does not make us timid, but gives us power, love and self-discipline."
~ 2 Timothy 1:7 (NIV: New International Version) ~

- **Perfection in your mind**: you obtain clarity in your thinking, a calmness in your thoughts; you have the ability to relax and sleep at night.

"We demolish arguments and every pretension that sets itself up against the knowledge of God, and we take captive every thought to make it obedient to Christ."
~ 2 Corinthians 10:5 (NIV: New International Version) ~

So girlfriend, know that in your times of trouble, God is at work, perfecting you, allowing you to be squeezed, so that endurance can be produced in your life.

You will emerge from this season, this trial, more beautiful and more glorious than ever before.

PRAYER FOR TODAY
Father, I thank you that even during the difficult times in my life you are at work in me - growing, developing and perfecting me - to become the person you pre-destined me to be. I know you will work all things out for my good and your glory. Amen.

DAY SEVEN
YOUR TIME IS NOW

"At the right time, I, the LORD, will make it happen"
Isaiah 60:22
(NLT: New Living Translation)

HOW TO BE BRAVE

God created time. He owns time. He's not restricted to or dictated by time, because He's outside of time. Time is set by Him.

But you and I *do* live within a timeframe. When you were born, you were gifted with a finite amount of time to spend on this earth. That time is our *life* or *lifetime* and it's precious.

Time is unearned and indefinite. Some use it wisely, every minute of it and every moment, whilst others waste days of their life. With every tick of the clock, another second, another minute, another moment has passed that we can never get back again.

So today, I encourage you to respect the time you've been given. Be generous with your gift. Use it to bless others. Be kind, considerate and understanding. Be intentional with it. Pause for a moment and consider: is what you're doing worth your time or wasting it? Learn from what you got wrong yesterday. See what you can amend today. If you've been hurt in the past, don't waste your time harbouring offence. Instead, forgive, let go, and use your time for healing and growing. Trust in the *'Author of Life'* to give you what you need, when you need it, at the right time.

I believe we can make time work for us, rather than living as one who is a slave to it. As we commit our ways, our plans and our days to God, He enables us to get done all that needs to be done with time to spare. In the book of Joshua, Israel was in a battle, fighting their enemies. Joshua was leading the army. They knew they would lose daylight as the sun went down and there would be a chance of being defeated. So Joshua prayed to the Lord and said, *"Let the sun stand still over Gibeon, and the moon over the valley of Aijalon."*

> *"So the sun stood still and the moon stayed in place until the nation of Israel had defeated its enemies."*
> *~ Joshua 10:13 (NLT: New Living Translation) ~*

What just happened? God extended time! They prayed and He answered. He made one single day longer than it ought to have been so that they would gain victory over the enemy.

In the book of Isaiah, there is a story about King Hezekiah who became very ill. God sent Isaiah the prophet to speak to the king to tell him to put his affairs in order, for he was about to die – not the kind of message you want to hear, right? As you can imagine, King Hezekiah was distraught at the news and it says he turned his face towards the wall and prayed. He wept bitterly and asked God to remember the honourable life that he had lived, how he had faithfully served God and walked in truth and integrity his whole life.

> *"Then the word of the Lord came to Isaiah: "Go and tell Hezekiah, This is what the Lord, the God of your father David, says: I have heard your prayer and seen your tears; I will add fifteen years to your life."*
> *~ Isaiah 38:4-5 (NIV: New International Version) ~*

What just happened? God extended time! He added more years onto the king's life because He heard the king's cry, saw his pure heart, listened to his prayer and had compassion towards him. Time listens to God. Time obeys God. So why not put the precious time you have into the hands of almighty God and see what He will do in you and through you?

PRAYER FOR TODAY
Father God, you are the gift-giver of time. Help me to be responsible for what you've given me. Help me to understand that when I submit my day to you, you allow me to get done all that I need to get done with grace and peace that is not of this world. Help me not to be a timewaster with negative thoughts and idle conversation, but instead to recognise that the clock is ticking and you have a purpose for me in my everyday living. So I invite you into every hour and every moment of my today. Amen.

DAY EIGHT
KNOW YOUR WORTH

> *"She is a woman of strength and mighty valor! She's full of wealth and wisdom. The price paid for her was greater than many jewels."*
> Proverbs 31:10
> (TPT: The Passion Translation)

HOW TO BE BRAVE

We have a favourite holiday spot in Turkey. I remember being there several years ago and a local Turkish farmer offered my husband four camels and fifteen sheep for me! I don't know what was more concerning: the fact that this strange man thought that I was only worth the trade of a few smelly animals, or the contemplative look on my husband's face before he finally answered, "No." (I seriously thought for a moment that he was going to swap me out!)

I don't know if you've ever felt *'less than'*: less than ordinary, less than average, less than the girl next door? Well, I have news for you. You were never meant to be a comparison to any other version of *woman*. You can only ever be compared to the blueprint that God drew up for you when He brought you into existence.

The Proverbs 31 woman is the ideal we can all aspire to. She is described as a woman of:

STRENGTH – strong, able to withstand much, mentally and emotionally.

MIGHTY VALOR – brave and courageous in the face of adversity.

FULL OF WEALTH – rich in love, kindness, patience and understanding.

WISDOM – she knows what to do with what she's got.

Then he goes on to say:
The price paid for her was more than many jewels.

Did you know that your value is extortionate? You are worth more than any amount of cattle or cash!

Yet, even though we know what God's Word says about us, there is often a niggle within us, a disconnect between the words we read and what we believe, a voice of doubt that begins to whisper, *'that's not how I see me.'*

Luke 15: 8-10 finds Jesus telling a story about a woman who had ten silver coins, but one went missing. Even though she still had nine coins left, the woman was concerned about the missing one and was intent on finding it so that her set of coins would be complete again. In her efforts to find and recover the one, she turns on the lamp and begins to sweep out her house.

When we hit seasons of feeling low – low self-worth, low self-image – it's a huge indicator that you too have lost something. In the same way that the woman lost one of her coins, you can lose treasure from the list in Proverbs 31:10. When you lose sight of just one of the attributes God created you with, you are unable to see yourself properly, the way God sees you.

Maybe you can identify. Maybe you would say of yourself, '*I used to have strength, but I just don't anymore. I used to be able to fight off negative thoughts. I used to be courageous. I used to be vigorous and passionate about my life, but right now in this season, I'm beaten! I'm weary, worn down and I feel like I've lost my* **strength***.*'

Or maybe you've lost your **wisdom** and you feel like you live life unsure about the direction to choose and what decisions to make.

You find yourself careless with your mouth, confused in your thinking, you seem to have lost the balance between right and wrong. Maybe as you're reading this, something else is popping into your mind and you know you've lost your **hope**, lost your **peace** or lost your **joy**.

Well, here's the good news. Anything that has been lost can be found if you know how to go about looking for it, and the woman in our story did just that. Firstly, she turns on her lamp. When we shine a light, it reveals what was already there, but in darkness, it was hidden. She picks up her broom and begins to sweep the house, getting rid of clutter and unnecessary rubbish, and sweeping away the dust that had accumulated over time.

When the light had been lit and the room had been cleared of all that should not have been there, she found her missing coin.

So girls, my question to you is this: how much do you want to find the thing you feel you've lost? Are you being intentional? Or have you become complacent and settled for life without it? You will never fully know the value of you if you do not pursue that which is missing from you. Your light is God's Word. So I encourage you – read your Bible. Read through books like:

- **Psalms** to know who God is to you.
- **Proverbs** to get wisdom and direction.
- Read books like **1 Corinthians** and **2 Corinthians** to learn about righteous living.

And as you read through it, you will have some '*ah-ha!*' moments, some '*light-on*' revelation moments as you begin to see what you could not see before. But remember, the light will also show you what needs to go, as it reveals the dust of **complacency** that has settled in your spirit, the dirt of **negativity** building up in the corners of your house, cobwebs of **regret**, debris of **remorse** and that **attitude** that has been quietly decaying in the dark.

As the light moves around your house (the depths of your soul), you're going to have to deal with what is illuminated, sweeping out the ugly and unwanted things that have sat there for years, and as you do you will discover your missing treasure. You will remember who you are and whose you are, and confidently declare, '*my worth is more than any number of jewels*.'

When you truly understand just how valuable you are, you will never allow anyone to lessen your worth again.

PRAYER FOR TODAY
Thank you Jesus, that my life was paid for by you and you have placed great worth and value on me. So, may I not be careless, may I not speak down about myself or have a low opinion of myself, for you thought I was worth giving your everything for. You have said of me that I am precious and valued, and worth more than precious jewels. Help me to view myself in the way that you see me. May I not talk down about or disregard myself, for I am not my own, but I belong to you. Amen.

DAY NINE

WHAT'S IN YOUR HAND

"May the favor of the Lord our God rest on us; establish the work of our hands for us— yes, establish the work of our hands." Psalm 90:17 (NIV: New International Version)

HOW TO BE BRAVE

The word establish means: to achieve permanent acceptance or recognition. Did you know that God wants to do something of great recognition in you and through you? When you give what you can into the hands of the one who equips you, He takes your ordinary and makes it extraordinary.

Let me tell you about a woman called Dorcas. You can read about her in the book of Acts 9:36-43. Dorcas lived in a town called Joppa, situated on the shores of the Mediterranean in the region of Palestine.

There was a church in Joppa. It is believed they quite possibly gathered for worship and prayer in the home of Dorcas.

We know very little about her - her age, position, title, whether she was married, divorced or widowed. The Bible doesn't disclose any of this information, but it is clear in verse 36 that *'she was always doing good and helping the poor.'*

Dorcas is described as a disciple of Jesus, which means a follower (in the truest sense of the word).

Did you know there is a difference between just being a Christian and being a disciple? A Christian accepts Jesus Christ as their personal Lord and saviour. A disciple is a (disciplined) follower of Christ, one who allows their lives to be challenged and shaped by the Word of God.

So it's possible for you to become a Christian but nothing changes in your life, or you can become a disciple and be transformed along the journey of following Jesus.

Dorcas believed in God and her discipleship was outworked through her love for people.

Dorcas was always doing good. She was a seamstress – she made clothes for the poor, repaired what was torn and worn, she made robes and wraps, scarves and skirts - all of this with no fancy machine to thread or foot pedal to operate. Dorcas had a needle; that was it, the smallest of instruments. But when you ask God to bless the little you have, to work through you, when you place your talent into His hands, He always makes it go further than it could have gone in your hands alone.

Remember the stories of old:

1 Kings 17:7-24 tells the story of a widow who had a little flour and oil, enough to make her last meal before she and her son died of starvation due to a three-year drought. But then Elijah the prophet, the man of God, met her at the town gate while she was gathering sticks and said, "*If you feed me first, you will never go hungry again*" (paraphrased). She put God first and He blessed her so that her little became a lot. Her '*jar of flour was not used up and the jug of oil did not run dry.*' Her supplies and produce never ran out again – every time she went to the kitchen cupboads they were full!

In **1 Samuel 17**, we find a boy called David amongst an army of thousands of armed and equipped men, none of whom would stand up to fight against a Philistine giant. This one boy had only a slingshot, a few stones and a humble prayer that said, "*God, this is all I have. But I know if you are for me, this is all I need.*" (paraphrased). He said to King Saul, "*The Lord who rescued me from the paw of the lion and the paw of the bear will rescue me from the hand of this Philistine.*" And with one shot he took down Goliath and changed the course of history forever.

In **Judges 4:17-19**, we meet Jael. All she had was a tent peg in her hand when the enemy came to her tent. But she believed she had the strength of Heaven behind her and used that tent peg to kill the commander of the army of the enemy who had been cruelly oppressing her people.
Our girl, Dorcas, had a needle and through the work of that needle in her hands, God used her mightily and many lives were blessed.

Your ministry is always through what you can already do. It's when your works are in the hands of God that what you're doing becomes so much more productive and effective.

However, there is a sudden turn of events in the story. Dorcas becomes ill and dies. This was a huge loss for this small community in Joppa. It just so happened that Peter, Jesus's disciple, was in the area at that time and he was asked to come to the house where Dorcas's body was laid out. The people who were mourning had all brought with them the garments that Dorcas had made for them. Dorcas had done so much for the people. She had gone above and beyond to serve with her little needle. As Peter prayed over Dorcas's body, the Spirit of God breathed life into her once again and Dorcas lived.

Just as it says in today's scripture, the favour of the Lord was upon her and the work of her hands was established through Him (paraphrased).

What do you have that you could serve others with?

The gift of encouragement? The gift of baking? Financial wisdom? A gift of teaching? The gift of cleaning? Whatever it is, when you use what you have to bless others, it attracts God's unmerited favour towards you. When we encourage others, God breathes life into areas of our life that once seemed dead.

PRAYER FOR TODAY

God, today I pray that you take my little, and in Your hands, I believe it can become much. Use me in my ordinary everyday life to help, bless and inspire others, knowing that as I live a giving life, it delights you. Thank you that you have purposed me to be a mighty influencer to those in my world. Amen.

DAY TEN
LISTEN TO THE ORIGINAL SAT NAV

"You're blessed when you stay on course, walking steadily on the road revealed by God. You're blessed when you follow his directions, doing your best to find him. That's right—you don't go off on your own; you walk straight along the road he set. You, God, prescribed the right way to live; now you expect us to live it. Oh, that my steps might be steady, keeping to the course you set; Then I'd never have any regrets in comparing my life with your counsel. I thank you for speaking straight from your heart; I learn the pattern of your righteous ways. I'm going to do what you tell me to do; don't ever walk off and leave me."
Psalm 119:1-8
(MSG: The Message)

HOW TO BE BRAVE

I think sat-navs were a God-inspired invention to help us better understand how the Holy Spirit works in our lives, how He prompts us to make decisions, shows us where we need to turn left and right, indicating what's ahead in the journey of life. He encourages us when we're on the right road and when we make wrong choices, He whispers, *'please turn around when possible.'*

God had a plan for your life before you ever came into being. His plan was not random, nor is it hidden to the point where you can't find it or follow it.

His plan is a greater purpose for your life. It is the preferred way for you to go. God wants you to succeed.

He wants to see you fulfilled. He wants your life to be prosperous and full, relationally, in your health, financially, practically, and academically. He intentionally reveals His plan for you to follow by what is written in His Word.

Now, I'm no good at baking, but I *can* follow a recipe. This I know: if I have all the right ingredients, the right equipment and a plan to follow, I can't go wrong. If I add the right ingredients, in the right order, at the right time, whether I think I'm good at baking or not is irrelevant because I'm going to produce a cake! If I follow the written instructions, I cannot go wrong.

Being committed to the ways of God, staying true to them no matter what season of life you are in, and loving Him with all of your heart, are your **ingredients**.

Belonging to and planting yourself in the local church is the **equipment** you need.

Reading and applying the Word of God daily is your **instruction**. This will show you what your life needs to flow – what to do, when to do it, and in what order – to produce the right results.

In **Judges 13:2-24**, we find ourselves introduced to a woman. Though her name is not directly mentioned in the Bible, an Encyclopedia of Jewish Women states *'the Babylonian Rabbis knew Manoah's wife as "Zlelponi" or "Zlelponith."'* This woman was the mother of Samson. She was barren – childless and desperate for a baby – and God heard her cry.

When we, as women, cry, it is often due to an area of barrenness in our lives, finding ourselves lacking in an area that we desperately want to be filled. We can find ourselves barren of love, barren of peace, barren of joy, barren in the area of friendship, barren of confidence. God knows the unproductive, unfruitful areas of your life – the areas that look dead, impossible and hopeless – where nothing has happened for years!

Now, right in the middle of Zlelponith's disappointment, God sends an angel to tell her that He has heard the cry of her heart. The angel says "I know that you are barren and childless, but you're going to become pregnant and bear a son. But take much care: *Drink no wine or beer; eat nothing ritually unclean. You are, in fact, pregnant right now, carrying a son.*"

Though Zlelponith could not see the answer, she fully believed that God had answered her prayers and therefore, in full faith, she took responsibility to follow what the angel requested of her, to drink no wine and eat nothing ritually unclean.

I think God was teaching her to exercise self-control. No matter what you see everyone else doing, remember you're carrying a promise on the inside of you.

For that promise to live, you need to:
- Control your mouth
- Control your thoughts
- Control your actions and know when to say "No!"

Consider what you are consuming. Gossip is contamination, taking offence is contamination, having a bad attitude is contamination. If you let these things in, they can harm the prayer incubating on the inside of you, leaving it unanswered. Seeds of promise will die when you're feeding on the wrong stuff.

As we read on in the story, we see Zlelponith telling her husband everything the angel told her. She was asking Manoah to hold her accountable. Although she carries the promise, she needed the support, wisdom, help, and positive influence of others, to bring it to full fruition.

You're blessed when you stay on course, walking steadily on the road revealed by God

PSALM 119:1-8

Find someone, a friend, or a good influence in your life, who loves God and loves you, but who also loves you enough to tell you when you're going wrong.

I can imagine Zlelponith saying to Manoah:

- *"If you see me having a glass of wine - take it out of my hand!"*
- *"If you see me with the pork sandwich - make me put it down!"*
- *"I'm giving you permission to be firm with me in an area that I know I may be weak"*
- *"I need your help so that all that is within me will grow to be healthy and strong"*

Who is there in your life that you have permitted to tell you when your attitude is off, who will tell you what you are saying sounds like gossip and you need to stop?

A child, in the natural, needs more than just a mother to bring them into the world and help them grow. It takes other sources of nurture (doctors, midwives, nutritionists, health visitors, friends and family etc.) to keep the mother on track and get that baby delivered safely.

Let's be women of wisdom who follow the order and pattern of the ways of God, and give birth to the incredible blessings He has promised to us.

PRAYER FOR TODAY
Lord, I believe that I'm carrying promise and purpose in my life, and although I may not see exactly what that is right now, I believe that you are growing something on the inside of me today that is going to be a blessing in my future. Help me to be wise and responsible, to nurture and protect the dream within, and allow the influence and wisdom of good godly leadership to help me bring it forth. Amen.

DAY ELEVEN
HOLD ON TO YOUR DREAM

HOW TO BE BRAVE

You might ask, "is it true that God could give me the desires of my heart?" Well, yes, it is!

But first, let's be clear about what a *true* God-given desire is by looking at what it is not. It is not flicking through a magazine and spotting a pair of designer shoes that you fancy. That's just a fleeting desire that lasts for a moment, an *'I wish I had them'* or *'I'd love to own them'* moment.

A true desire is a longing, an aching, in your heart – to do, to achieve, to become or obtain something – that you just can't seem to get over or move past. God specialises in giving you the desires of your heart because most often it was He who put them there in the first place. He places desires on the inside of you to cause you to long after his purpose for your life.

You know if what you desire is God-given, because it consumes you. You dream about it when you're awake. You keep thinking and imagining what it will be like when it becomes a reality in your life.

> *"Delight yourself in the Lord and he will give you the desires of your heart."*
> *Psalm 37:4*
> *(ESV: English Standard Version)*

Albert Einstein is reported to have said, *'Imagination is everything. It is the preview of life's coming attractions.'* It's kind of like seeing the trailer of a movie before you see the whole movie. The trailer gives you a preview of what to expect and although you haven't seen the whole film yet, you've had a glimpse, a snapshot of what's to come so you can get excited about it.

When God puts His desire in you, the coming days, weeks and sometimes years that follow, will often give you a foretaste of what the future could look like. You may find yourself leaning towards certain people, or drawn to a certain place. You will find yourself thinking thoughts you just can't shake off and may even start speaking a certain way because every fibre of your being is preparing for who you are becoming, for the 'one day when' the dream finally becomes a reality.

Another way to recognise if the thing you desire is God inspired is when it seems almost impossible. If the dream were possible, you would have probably gone ahead and made it happen by now yourself. You wouldn't need God's help to make it happen and you wouldn't still be praying so hard for it.

A God breathed desire doesn't mean that God is just going to give it to you though. You're going to have to work too. God most often works in partnership with us, which means you do all that you can do and God will do the impossible. There are going to be times when it feels like it is never going to happen. There will be days when you feel like you're moving further away from your goal rather than closer to it.

There will be times when you feel disappointed and disheartend, but remember, it took Thomas Edison a thousand unsuccessful attempts to create a light bulb before he finally got it right. He is reported to have said, *'Many of life's failures are people who did not realize how close they were to success when they gave up.'*

I want to encourage you today, never give up hoping for and believing for those deepest desires, the longings that God has put on the inside of you. He is the God of perfect timing and He will bring it to pass if you stay persistent. Think about it: He has our planet spinning at just the right speed so that it stays in the right place and we all stay on it! He knows how to work all things in a perfect and timely fashion, so if you can trust Him to keep the earth spinning at just the right speed, you sure can trust Him with your dream. If you haven't yet seen your dream become a reality, then perhaps it's simply not yet your time. Perhaps it's not God's timing. But one day it will be. So, on the days when you feel disheartened like it's never going to happen for you, be mindful that in your waiting He's still working.

There is a roller-coaster kind of a story to be found in **2 Kings 4** about the prophet Elisha, a representative of God, and a Shunammite woman. She has a secret dream to become a mother one day. But the older she became in years, the further this dream felt from ever becoming a reality. We can learn a lesson from this woman's life. While she was waiting, the woman from Shunem was serving.

As the years rolled by, she must have felt the pain of disappointment that she had still not yet conceived. I'm sure that at times, life felt cruel and unfair to her. In Biblical times, there could be a sense of shame and social stigma for women who struggled to get pregnant. We don't know her name or her exact age. We don't know much about her marriage or her work. But we do know that she was 'well to do' and that she didn't sit around and pity her situation. Instead, she found ways to practically bless the 'holy man of God.'

Elisha often passed through her town to minister and she knew that she could offer him hospitality. So she and her husband opened up their home to Elisha and furnished a bedroom at the top of the house for him to stay in. The Bible doesn't say, but it may well have been a room that she had set aside to be a nursery for the child she longed for. She decided to turn her disappointment into an opportunity.

Instead of leaving the room empty because of her unfulfilled dreams, she filled it with purpose and made space for the presence of God.

And so Elisha would come and stay at her house. She cooked for him, cleaned for him and allowed him to rest in the very room where she should have been nursing her dream, never once complaining about her disappointment.

So when we are in seasons of waiting, perhaps feeling like our dream is not working out, dealing with the pain and regret that comes with it, maybe our attitude should be one of, 'I'm going to help someone else out and fill the void of my disappointment with the purposes of God.' Because when you can love on another person when you are feeling unloved yourself, when you give to another when you feel you are in need, when you are generous with your actions and intentions even when you feel you've been overlooked, that is one of the bravest things you can do. In fact, you are serving God and 'delighting yourself in Him.'

In other words, your relationship with God is not based on what you do or do not have. It is based on the knowledge that, though life hasn't gone the way you thought that it would, He is God, and He is good, regardless of our situation.

The promise attached to an attitude like that is this: '**He will give you the desires of your heart**.' You can read the story for yourself in 2 Kings 4:8-37. Although she never dared to ask Elisha for blessing, he blessed her anyway. The Shunammite woman did conceive and she gave birth to a long-awaited son.

So to every woman who is in a place of waiting right now, whatever your desire is – to be married, healed, debt-free, waiting for a baby, a fresh start in life,waiting for an apology or waiting for reconciliation – remember that when you get busy with what's on God's heart, He will get busy with yours.

PRAYER FOR TODAY

Lord God, help me to see that you are a God of abundant blessing and all I ever need to be complete in this life is found in you. In this waiting season, I give myself to serve you, in whatever way or form that looks like, for your glory. Use me to be a blessing to others while I confidently wait for my dreams and desires to come to fruition. Amen.

Hold on To Your dreams

DAY TWELVE
WORK YOUR WONKY

> "Oh yes, you shaped me first inside, then out; you formed
> me in my mother's womb."
> *Psalms 139:13 (MSG: The Message)*

HOW TO BE BRAVE

Several years ago, a new label appeared on our supermarket shelves in the produce aisle: it read '*Wonky Fruit*.' The fruit and veg sporting these labels were slightly different in appearance than our usual fruit and veg. They were shaped differently, not uniformed like regular fruit. Perhaps they were not quite as clean and their colour was sometimes dull compared to the nicely packaged bright red tomatoes and strawberries on the shelves besides them. The list of oddities went on.

I decided to purchase some of our '*wonky*' friends as they seemed far better value for money than regular fruits and veg. I remember arriving home from that particular grocery shop and rapidly washing, peeling and chopping my '*wonky*' purchase before my judgemental family could say, "*Ugh, I'm not eating that!*"

Wanting to double-check that what I'd bought still had all the nutritional value of regular fruit and veg, I did a little research. I came across an article, from The Independent, that informed me that '*wonky*' food can also go by another name – '*Ugly Veg*.' It reported that in 2013, '*ugly*' or '*wonky*' fruit and veg were blamed for up to 40 per cent of wasted fruit and vegetables. A significant amount of food was being wasted or discarded on aesthetic or cosmetic grounds – it didn't look nice enough.

Apparently, the way we're attracted to other humans also seems to apply to our food. We often judge by appearance first. Human attraction often goes like this: the more beautiful a person is in appearance, the more intelligent, honest and successful we presume they are. So we're naturally attracted to these people. We appear to eat with our eyes before we do with our mouths. So the colour, shape, size and display of our food can either appeal to us or repulse us before we've even given it a try.

In order to grow perfect fruit and veg worthy of reaching the supermarket shelf standards, farmers often have to resort to using chemicals and cosmetic pesticides to grow their produce. However, these pesticides can stay as a residue on food and also negatively affect the environment.

Think about that for a moment – the straighter the carrot and the brighter its colour or the more perfectly formed a strawberry is – it's taken more chemical enhancement to achieve that look. Though they appear perfect on the outside, they are in fact less nutritious on the inside. So the truth is, wonkier misshapen fruit and veg are actually better for us.

Even though I was reading articles about food, I couldn't help but see the similarities in the way we look at and judge people. We live in a society where pressure is constantly placed on us to live up to the world's standards of what is *'normal'* or *'acceptable'*, a world where nothing less than perfect will do. From the features on your face to the measurement of your waist, we judge one another by outward appearance. We spend our days competing and comparing, conforming and trying to fit in. Yet we fail to see that we are measuring ourselves by the wrong type of measure, for the way the world views you is very different to the way that God sees you.

In **1 Samuel 10**, when the Israelite nation was looking for a king, the people chose Saul to lead them. Saul looked like the perfect king from the outside when judged by the world's standards. He was tall and good-looking; he looked the way a king should look. But there was something not quite right on the inside.

In **1 Samuel 13:8-14**, Saul disobeys God and makes an illegal sacrifice. Samuel, the priest, says to him, "Y*ou have done foolishly. You have not kept the command of the Lord your God, with which he commanded you. For then the Lord would have established your kingdom over Israel forever. But now your kingdom shall not continue."*

Over the course of time it is revealed that Saul's character is flawed. He is not *'a man after (God's) own heart'* at all, but instead, he was a jealous and disobedient man, full of pride, so God chooses another king to take Saul's place. He sends Samuel to the house of Jesse, as one of his sons is to be anointed future king over Israel.

First, Samuel sees Eliab, and he thinks to himself, *'surely this is the Lord's anointed,'* because, just like Saul, he looked as a king should look on the outside. But Samuel hears God say, "*Do not look on his appearance or on the height of his stature, because I have rejected him. For the Lord sees not as man sees: man looks on the outward appearance, but the Lord looks on the heart.*"

It is *actually* David, the youngest son, who was initially overlooked, left out in the field tending to his father's sheep, whom God chooses to be anointed as the next king. David is believed to be the author of our scripture today, taken from **Psalm 139**.

The Lord is not concerned with outer appearances and how we look, but he is focused on who we are becoming.

We're all created to be individual and unique and yet we've allowed ourselves to be deceived into measuring ourselves against our sisters' version of '*normal*' or '*perfection*'. We spend our days competing with each other and comparing our lives to theirs, wishing we looked like them, wishing we could have what they have or could do what they do. We have allowed feelings of inferiority to dominate our thoughts and it's time to fix your focus on something higher.

We've looked at how '*wonky*' fruits can appear to be less than. They are not perfect by the world's standards, but they're packed with nutrients that are beneficial to the health of your body.

The same applies to you, it's what's in you that matters. You were designed to be a blessing to others and to be beneficial to the world around you!

You're not just the best version of you that there will ever be, but you are the only version of you that there will ever be. No one else has your footprint or fingerprint, not even if you're an identical twin. God doesn't make duplicates or replicas of someone from thousands of years ago. He created you and chose you to be who you truly are *'for such a time as this'*.

He designed you in such a way that you are perfectly formed and equipped to live out the life He has purposed for you.

When the Psalmist writes about being shaped inside first, he's not just referring to your skeletal system or the organs working inside your body. He is also referring to the uniqueness of your DNA and character.

Everything about you is purposeful and special. Pastor Rick Warren has a beautiful and easy way to remember that we were created with a unique SHAPE, an acrostic that stands for:

- Spiritual Gifts
- Heart
- Abilities
- Personality
- Experiences

You can read more about them on his website, '*PastorRick.com*' and in his book '*The Purpose Driven Life.*'

Your gift is unique. It's that thing you're just good at without even trying. For some people, it may be an obvious gift, like music or singing. For others, it might be the gift of hospitality or generosity. We all have at least one gift and if you're not sure what yours is yet, then just pause or take a moment and think. Maybe you're good with words, mathematics or looking after children. All these things are a gift given to you from God that can bless the people around you.

Your heart has a unique shape. It's the things you're passionate about, the things that make you tick, things you just love to do! These things make you uniquely you. You have a unique personality. That's a part of your shape too. We are all different. Some people are loud and others are quiet, there are introverts and others are extroverts. Some people are loud criers and others are silent criers. There are charismatic folk and then others who are completely subdued.

We all have our own personal expressions and experiences of life so far and these are unique to you. They are the very best and the very worst things that you've been through. They are the lessons you've learnt on the journey so far, your highlights and your darkest moments, your ups and downs. But God uses all of your life to define you and shape you, and nothing gets wasted in His hands.

It takes a brave woman to live authentically, living out her individuality. It takes a strong woman to choose not to compete and compare.

It takes a determined woman to be satisfied with running in her own lane, without allowing her mind to waver and wander to what other people are doing. But a woman of this kind will be seen by her God, even if she goes unrecognised by the world or by the people around her.

PRAYER FOR TODAY
Lord, today I ask that you help me to appreciate who I am, who you've created me to be. Help me to take my eyes off other people's talents and giftings, and fix my eyes on you – my maker and creator – the one who knows me better than I know myself. I am fearfully and wonderfully made to be me, created in your likeness and your image. So give me the courage, Lord, to boldly live out who you've called me to be. Amen.

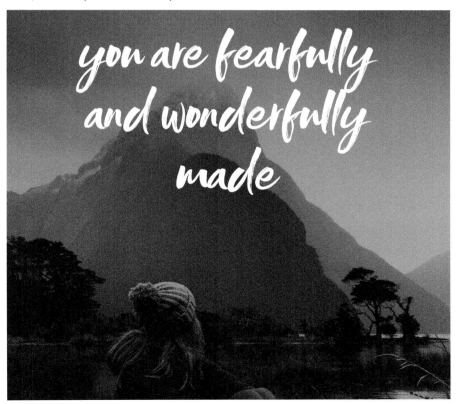

PART TWO

HOW TO SPEAK BRAVE

DAY THIRTEEN
CHECK YOUR 'BUILDER'S BUM'

> *"Guard your heart above all else, for it determines the course of your life."*
> *Proverbs 4:23*
> *(NLT: New Living Translation)*

HOW TO SPEAK BRAVE

I'm sure we are all familiar with the expression *'a builder's bum'*! It's when the builder who is working on some form of construction project exposes way more of himself than we need to see! The point being when your pants are slack, you reveal more than you mean to!

As we journey through life we become builders. We are busy constructing relationships, building careers, building a family, friendships, and a reputation, to name but a few areas. And we, like a builder in the natural, can become careless and expose ourselves in ways we don't want to be seen.

When complacency creeps into your life, you stop caring about what you're wearing. Did you know you wear more than just clothes? You wear your mood. You wear an attitude. What you reveal of your character shows what you have chosen to wear today.

The word '**complacency**' means: to have an uncritical satisfaction of yourself. In other words, you stop putting effort into you, although you may be aware of areas of your life that need attention, traits in your character that are slightly off. You just begin to coast along with the mentality of *'it doesn't really matter. I'm doing just fine.'*

When you stop caring about what you wear in the natural, you no longer do a check in front of the mirror before you leave the house. It's only by looking at your reflection in the mirror that you can spot buttons that are misaligned, see the stains on your clothes you didn't know were there, or that the top you've chosen to put on clashes with your bottom half. The same thing happens to you on the inside when you stop using the Word of God as a spiritual *'mirror,'* allowing it to reflect back to you the emotion or the mindset you are wearing today.

So when complacency creeps into your life, you slacken the areas you ought to be keeping a close guard on.

You expose a side of yourself that you didn't mean for others to see. You reveal a bad attitude. You expose yourself with a critical comment.

Luke 6:45 reminds us that whatever is in our heart will eventually come out of our mouth: *'for the mouth speaks what the heart is full of.'*

The heart of a person can be exposed just like the *'builder's bum'*. We are supposed to guard our heart, to protect it, not allowing jealousy, anger, pride and other negative emotions to dwell there. But when we become slack, unforgiveness creeps in, wrong mindsets form, and the way we've been thinking on the inside is now revealed on the outside when we open our mouth.

Here's the thing: no one ever tells the builder that his unsightly buttocks are peeping over the top of his pants! He just carries on with his work whilst everyone else is talking about him. So you have to keep an eye on your pants to see what you're revealing!

You have to keep vigilant over the issues of your own heart. Keep *the belt of truth* (from Ephesians 6:14) tight around you, and keep your heart well-guarded.

One of the ways you can do this is by asking someone who knows you, *"how am I doing?"*. Ask someone who you know will be truthful with you even if it hurts, someone who is further on than you in their walk of faith, whom you trust.

In this season of my life, whilst I'm building my marriage, career, friendship circles and ministry, I need to ask myself, regularly:
- How am I doing?
- Are there any areas I could tighten up on?
- Am I slacking in any area and therefore revealing an unsightly part of my character?
- Have I exposed myself in my attitude?
- Have I been careless with my mouth and shown something ugly in my heart?

Ask yourself a question: Am I building my life on random decisions or am I building it with precision?

Random decision-making means living every day as it comes, doing what we want to do, without much thought as to why we're doing it, saying what we think without thinking about what we say. It's loving life in such a way that you do not give much consideration to the consequences.

On the other hand, a life built with *precision* is a life aimed towards a target. I know who I want to become and I know what I want to achieve. I have dreams and ambitions and I'm going to tailor every area of my life towards that goal. I'm going to keep my heart guarded, using the Word of God as a mirror every day to reflect my heart back to me.

I'm keeping my belt tight, so that my conduct, character and countenance are working in a right and pleasing way, taking me closer towards my desired destination and the person I see myself becoming tomorrow.

Every one of us, at some time or another, has acted in a way we wish we hadn't. We have all been careless with our mouths or thoughtless with our actions. But once we recognise how easily we can expose ourselves, we then have to take responsibility to keep guard over ourselves.

Our scripture for today says we are to guard our heart '*above all else*.' These are strong words.

'*Above all else*' means:

above socialising, entertaining, shopping, working, your university assignment, above your gathering and partying, above the latest news report or social media feeds, above other beliefs, opinions and standards. **ABOVE ALL ELSE!**

The first thing I will do every morning and the last thing I do every evening is to set a guard over the doorway of my heart. I will be vigilant over what I watch because I know what my eyes behold enters my heart. I will wisely choose the company I keep as those who influence me also influence the issues of my heart. I will think about what I listen to because music and conversation change the atmosphere around me. I have come to fully understand, girls, that as you keep vigilant over your own heart daily, it will direct your mouth and you become trustworthy in the eyes of God a magnetic to the blessings from God.

PRAYER FOR TODAY

I pray that I will become wise and vigilant in protecting my heart, Lord. I understand that my life is guided by the activity of my heart and I desire your goodness and your blessing on the rest of my life. So I earnestly pray for you to help me put you first and protect the ways in which my heart is influenced. Amen.

DAY FOURTEEN
A DISCERNING WOMAN

"O Lord, listen to my cry; give me the discerning mind you promised"
Psalm 119:169 (NLT: New Living Translation)

HOW TO SPEAK BRAVE

Did you know that God has put wisdom, authority, power and discernment within you, a woman? We are not upon the earth to compete with other people, but rather to assist, complement and add to the world through the gift that is womanhood, and part of that gift is the ability to discern a little differently.

'**Discernment**' means the ability to judge well, an act of perceiving or understanding something, the quality of being able to grasp and comprehend what is obscure.

We just see things differently, right?

There is a comical myth or stereotype that a man views the world in binary, like a black and white TV. But the same world viewed through the lens of a woman has all sorts of colours and details, more like a HD TV.

I believe the ability to see the world in colourful detail carries over into our faith life too. We love differently, we pray differently (often giving God incredible amounts of detail about the situation we're praying for – as if He doesn't already know!)

God loves a passionate woman, someone who is determined to hear from Him, pushing for an answer, intent on getting a result. She hasn't slept, she hasn't eaten, her prayers are not articulated particularly well, but they are loud and tear-soaked. She half-sings them, half-shouts them.

She looks like a woman going to war – but oh! – the Lord hears her.

Her tears speak a volume of detail without her words even forming.
The noise from her mouth may make no sense to the human ear, but when

they are heard in the unseen realm, hell's gates are shaken and Heaven's doors are opened. The sound of a woman makes the enemy tremble and release what he's been holding over her.

Friend, you and I were given a voice with a full range of octaves so we can influence the world with our sound. We can change the tempo, alter the atmosphere, grab hold of faith and diminish fear, all with the sound of our voice.

There is a time to speak softly, a time to whisper, a time to speak love and a time to be gentle. There is a time to be silent and a time to be loud. There is a time to shout out and cry out and let the enemy know you will fight for the promise of God over your life and that of your family.

In **2 Samuel 20:16-22**, we find a woman who opened her mouth and shouted at those who were threatening her city. Though the Bible doesn't give us her name, she was described as '*a wise woman*.'

The villain of the story is a 'troublemaker' called Sheba, who was leading a revolt against King David. Word had reached the king that Sheba and his army were hiding in a walled city called Abel Beth Maakah. David deployed 'his mighty warriors' to attack the city.

So think about this. The citizens of the city do not know that there is a fugitive hiding amongst them. They are carrying out their everyday business, trading in the marketplace, coming and going from their homes, farming their land, doing the school run and housework as normal, when suddenly the guard on lookout raises the alarm – "the city is under siege!" (paraphrased).

Thousands of soldiers had surrounded the walls and were attacking the city. '*All the troops with Joab came and besieged Sheba in Abel Beth Maakah. They built a siege ramp up to the city, and it stood against the outer fortifications.*'

Just then, as if out of nowhere, a woman appears on the scene. We do not know her name, the bible simply describes her as 'one wise woman' and she has discernment in this whole situation. The men are on a mission to capture the perpetrator by attacking the entire city. But the woman sees the detail they are missing. She begins to think about the innocent people that would be caught up in the bloodshed, how hundreds of lives would be lost in a massacre, children killed, cattle slaughtered, homes burned to the ground.

So this woman rolls up her sleeves, takes off her apron, and climbs to the top of the city wall and shouts, "**Oi! Who's in charge here? I have something to say.**" (paraphrased)

In front of thousands of testosterone-fuelled angry men outside the wall and hysterical innocent bystanders inside the wall, with no microphone or amplification, there was a God-given authority in her voice that brought thousands of men to a halt!

I believe that when you do all that you can do, God will carry your voice right into the camp of your oppressor. What do you have that you could serve others with?

The whole operation came to a standstill because one woman raised her voice in the right direction. Her words carried wisdom. Her language had an authority in it that brought a sense of calm so that law and order could be restored. Her wise actions brought resolution to the problem without blood-shed. No army was needed, just the capture of one bad man, all negotiated by one wise woman.

Joab explains the situation and says, "Hand over this one man, and I'll withdraw from the city," to which she replies, "His head will be thrown to you from the wall."

This woman went and found Sheba, cut off his head and tossed it over the wall to the awaiting army. With courage and confidence she single handedly made happen peaceably what thousands of men could not.

The moral of the story is this: You have a voice that God wants you to use upon the earth today.

He wants to use your voice to bring resolve, calm conflict, speak wisdom, and speak up for the innocent. He needs you to open your mouth and bring order to the chaos. If this woman had pondered and thought about what she was going to do, it would have been too late and the opportunity to make a difference would have passed.

So often, we talk ourselves out of doing the very thing that we feel God is asking us to do because we think *'who am I that anyone should listen? As if my voice could make a difference!'*

Let me remind you, God created you to see differently so that you could be a difference-maker. You, who can see the detail of justice, who knows the promises of peace, will you be the one to let out a shout and declaration of praise? Are you the one who will open her mouth so that the truth can be heard in your home, in your workplace and echoing from your church?

- You can open your mouth and move that mountain!
- You can find your voice and shift that problem!
- You were made to be loud!
- You were made to be noticed!

May hell's gates tremble and Heavens doors open at the sound of your obedient voice today!

PRAYER FOR TODAY
Lord, open my eyes to see things the way you see them. May I speak out loud your goodness and have the boldness to speak wisdom into my home, my workplace, my friendships, and all the different areas of my life. Use me to diffuse problems and be a peace-maker where there is strife. Thank you forgiving me eyes that see detail and for a heart of compassion. Amen.

DAY FIFTEEN
DON'T SETTLE FOR AVERAGE

"When they arrived at Bethsaida, some people brought a blind man to Jesus, and they begged him to touch the man and heal him. Jesus took the blind man by the hand and led him out of the village. Then, spitting on the man's eyes, he laid his hands on him and asked, "Can you see anything now?" The man looked around. "Yes," he said, "I see people, but I can't see them very clearly. They look like trees walking around." Then Jesus placed his hands on the man's eyes again, and his eyes were opened. His sight was completely restored, and he could see everything clearly."
Mark 8:22-25
(NLT: New Living Translation)

HOW TO SPEAK BRAVE

I don't know if you've ever asked God for healing in an area of your life. It may have been in your physical body, as it was for the blind man in our text today. Or it may have been in another area of your life, maybe a relationship that needed healing or emotional trauma you've experienced.

There are all sorts of areas in life where we need the healing power of Jesus:

- Healing in our mind (including from thoughts that control us or limit us).
- Healing in our friendships and relationships.
- Healing in our finances.
- Things we've lost and need restoring to us (like our dignity or our confidence).

Two things stand out to me from this story; Firstly, Jesus *spat* on the man's eyes! (ew, gross I know!) What He did was outrageous and unexpected. I think Jesus was teaching this man and those watching, not to put him in a box or try to predict how He would work. I can imagine Him saying, "You asked me for healing. But how I do it may just surprise you, because I will work in ways that you won't recognise or appreciate." (Nobody appreciates being spat on, right?)

The blind man didn't pull back, he didn't question what Jesus was doing. He simply had the faith to believe Jesus could restore what he'd lost.

It's your faith in God that makes way for the miracle.

Although what is happening right now may not look the way I imagined God would work, I still believe He's healing me because I've asked Him to. Even though I don't understand it and I can't see or feel it, I'm not going to question Him and I'm still going to trust Him.

"Now to Him who is able to [carry out His purpose and] do superabundantly more than all that we dare ask or think [infinitely beyond our greatest prayers, hopes, or dreams], according to His power that is at work within us…"
~ Ephesians 3:20 (AMP: Amplified Bible) ~

What if **superabundantly more** means stranger, wilder, crazier, unimaginable things too? Will you still trust Him?

Secondly, Jesus touched the blind man's eyes and asked him if he could see. The blind man said, "*Yes, but not clearly*." So Jesus touched him again.

The man could have settled for *okay*. He could have said, 'A little fuzzy sight is better than no sight, so I'll just settle for what I've got.' But he didn't settle for just *okay*.

So often we've settled for *okay*. We pray for God to intervene and turn our situation around and when it gets a little better, when things are slightly improved, we stop there:

- I'm married, it's a loveless marriage – but it's *okay*
- I have a job, it's a dead-end job with no prospects – but it's *okay*
- I'm better than I used to be but I'm not completely well – but I'm *okay*
- I have kids, they're not speaking to me – but it's *okay*!

It is not okay!

If partial sight was not okay for the blind man in our story, then why should 'partial anything' be okay with you? He had the boldness and confidence toinvite Jesus to touch him a second time. When Jesus touched him a second time he was fully restored!

Partial sight is not the answer he wanted from a God who has promised to give us '*infinitely beyond our greatest prayers, hopes and dreams*.'

I think sometimes God waits to see how much we really want the thing we're asking for.

If you're single and hoping to be married one day, will any guy do? Or are you being specific about the type of man you're praying for, his morals, his character, his lifestyle?

If you need healing in your body, mind or spirit, are you generalising in your prayer for healing, or are you being specific and telling God exactly where you need your health to be restored?

Don't settle for a halfway life. God is a loving and generous father who wants to lavish blessings on us while we are here on earth. As I said earlier, sometimes I think He wants to see how much we really want the thing we've been asking for. Are we going to give up seeking Him when we've got a little? Or are we going to confidently pray until we see full restoration and complete healing in that area of our life?

So speak up and speak out for a full miracle! Don't settle for any less.

PRAYER FOR TODAY
Dear Lord, I know you are an 'above and beyond' generous God. Your Word tells me that no good thing will you withhold from me because you love me. So, if you are the God who never gives up on me, help me to be the kind of person who never gives up on you. May I always believe you can do it and trust your methods even when I don't understand how. Amen.

DAY SIXTEEN

GET YOUR VOICE BACK

> *"Sing, barren woman, you who never bore a child; burst into song, shout for joy, you who were never in labor; because more are the children of the desolate woman than of her who has a husband," says the Lord."*
> *Isaiah 54:1*
> *(NIV: New International Version)*

HOW TO SPEAK BRAVE

I've always found it slightly odd that the words *'sing'* and *'barren'* would be found in the same sentence. The word *'sing'* suggests joy and happiness; it has a feel-good factor to it. We sing when we are happy, right?

The word *'barren'*, on the other hand, describes a state of destitution, bleakness or brokenness. It is an area of life that is dry, parched or empty, where nothing grows and nothing seems to be productive. We looked at this before on Day 10 when we looked at how desperate Samson's mother was to have a baby.

We can experience barren times in our singleness or marriages, in our health, or finances. We can experience seasons of barrenness when there is strain or breakdown in our relationships with spouses, children, family and friends. We can all feel loneliness and isolation at times. Or maybe you've felt flat in your faith, limited in your prayer life or disengaged from church? These are all indications that maybe you're in a barren season.

Sometimes we know exactly how and why we arrived at these places. Yet there are times when we just seem to land there without any rhyme or reason.

Barrenness has a way of consuming us. Every waking moment of every day is drawn to that problem, that issue, that area of unanswered prayer. And yet within our scripture today, God has given us a Kingdom principle that makes no sense to our natural mind, but it is a powerful weapon to be used in your faith that will produce radical results in your life. And that weapon is to sing.

It's almost like God is setting us a challenge. Sing when you're broken, sing when it hurts, sing when it's all falling apart, sing when you've got nothing, sing when you're empty - open your mouth, my dear girl, and sing!

Now I don't know how it is for you, but when I open my mouth to sing it's not a very delightful sound that comes out. But that's okay because the word '*sing*' in this context doesn't necessarily mean to make a pleasant tune. '*Sing*' means to make a sound. The Amplified Bible translation of the same scripture replaces the word '*sing*' with '*shout*.' This is great for me! Though I may not be able to hold a tune, I can certainly let out a shout of praise!

When God created you, he put a sound deep down on the inside of you that is unique to you. No one else can make your sound except you. When you open your mouth to sing praises to Him, when you shout for joy, you release an audible sound from your mouth. But you also release another vibration into the atmosphere, one that is unheard with natural ears but heard by a supernatural God. Our God hears the sound of faith.

Modern-day science is establishing the theory that '*all things in our universe are constantly in motion, vibrating. Even objects that appear to be stationary are in fact vibrating, oscillating, resonating, at various frequencies*'.

But with you, He didn't just want to give you a sound. He gave you a voice and a choice. No other living matter can connect with God using their voice quite like you can. Scripture tells us that we were created in the image and the likeness of God, so could it be that when you open your mouth in praise to Him or prayerfully articulate your requests to Him, that God recognises something of himself in your sound?

If you are familiar with the Disney movie '*The Little Mermaid*,' you may remember the scene where the villainous sea monster, Ursula, convinces Ariel to give up her most treasured possession to gain the freedom of living on dry land and pursue the love of her life, Prince Eric. She gives up her voice.

Ariel has an enchanting and powerful voice and Prince Eric who lives on the land has fallen in love with this beautiful sound from the ocean. But to get closer to him, Ariel allows the wicked sea creature, Ursula, to take her voice in exchange for transforming her fishtail into legs. Sadly, all of Ariel's efforts to get close to her prince seem to fail for without her voice Eric doesn't recognise her as it was the sound of her voice he was drawn to, and her sweet song he had fallen in love with.

Like Ariel, we too have a deceitful Ursula in our lives, the devil. The bible describes him as a liar and a thief, who wants to silence you by taking your voice from you.

How does he do that? He tries to convince you that:

- Your barren places are too dry and will never see rain again.
- Your situation is too desperate and there is no hope.
- There is no point in opening your mouth to God anymore as He's not interested in you and not even listening.

And so you go silent, you remain quiet, and all the while Heaven is waiting and your father is listening. I imagine Him asking the questions, "Where are you? Why haven't I heard my daughter's voice in a while? Where is she, the one that I love?"

It takes bravery to push through discouragement. It takes a brave woman to sing, worship and pray when life seems to be falling apart. But you can do it. Just open your mouth and let your sound out, even if it makes no sense or has no tune, *'for out of the abundance of the heart [your] mouth speaks.'*

There are answers for the questions and concerns that you have you've stored up in your heart. When you open your mouth God hears your sound. As your faith is released, He's working on the answer, healing the pain and preparing your future.

Maybe you're not sure what should come out of your mouth when you open it. Do you wonder, *'what sort of sound should I be making*?' That's a great question to ask. Not every sound we make is appealing to God.

When we murmur and complain, when we constantly talk about what's wrong in our lives, that's not the sound of faith God is listening for.

God hears the voice of gratitude, even though there is still lack. He hears the voice that's worshipping Him, even during the problem you're facing. He hears the scripture you're reading, even though inwardly you're breaking. He hears the love you pour on Him in prayer, even though you feel low about yourself like no one cares.

In other words, He hears a broken life that is declaring, "I'm not prepared to wait until everything's great before I praise you. I'm praising you now, in my mess, in my brokenness, in advance of what I believe you're going to do for me."

Here are **ten daily declarations** of faith that you can speak out to remind yourself - "*I have a voice and I have a choice, and today I am choosing to let my voice be heard as I declare*"

- **Philippians 4:19**, "And my God will meet all [my] needs according to the riches of his glory in Christ Jesus."
- **Isaiah 54:17**, "No weapon forged against [me] will prevail, and [I] will refute every tongue that accuses [me]"
- **Deuteronomy 28:13**, "The Lord will make [me] the head, not the tail…"
- **Isaiah 45:2**, "[My God] will go before [me] and will level the mountains."
- **Isaiah 14:27**, "For the Lord Almighty has purposed, and who can thwart him? His hand is stretched out, and who can turn it back?"
- **Numbers 6:24-26**, "The Lord [will] bless [me] and keep [me]; the Lord [will] make his face to shine upon [me] and be gracious to [me]; the Lord [will] lift up his countenance upon [me] and give [me] peace."
- **Proverbs 18:21**, "Death and life are in the power of the tongue," so today I choose to speak life!
- **Romans 8:37**, "In all these things [I am] more than [a conqueror] through him who loved us."
- **Mark 9:23**, "All things are possible for one who believes," Lord, today I believe!
- **Matthew 21:22**, "Whatever [I] ask in prayer, [I] will receive, if [I] have faith," Lord, today I am asking in prayer for _____. I believe I will receive it.

PRAYER FOR TODAY
Lord, may the sound of my voice come before you today. May it be a sound that captures your attention as I raise my praise and plant my hope in you. Help me to remain faithful, believing that your promises are for my life, just as you are forever faithful, staying true to your Word. My voice is a gift from you. Please give me the strength to use your gift wisely. Amen.

DAY SEVENTEEN
YOU CAN CHANGE THE ATMOSPHERE

"To all who mourn in Israel, he will give a crown of beauty for ashes, a joyous blessing instead of mourning, festive praise instead of despair. In their righteousness, they will be like great oaks that the LORD has planted for his own glory."
Isaiah 61:3
(NLT: New Living Translation)

HOW TO SPEAK BRAVE

Many years ago, when we didn't have the technology that we have today before the world went digital, people would listen to music on a wireless radio. But trying to get a clear signal without interference was often tricky. You would have to tweak it, adjust it, and reposition the aerial constantly. In between all the adjusting, there was a lot of static noise, hissing and crackling. But as you turned the dial, eventually the frequency of the radio receiver would match the frequency of the signal being transmitted by the radio station and you would get a clearer sound.

Did you know that when we open our mouths in worship to God we are creating a spiritual frequency? As we push through our problems and get past our negative thoughts, we are tweaking our spirit until eventually our frequency matches that of God, and His will and His way become clearer to us.

2 Kings 24 marks the beginning of the end of the southern kingdom of Israel called '*Judah*'. King Nebuchadnezzar of Babylon attacked the nation. The Babylonians destroyed Solomon's temple in Jerusalem and ravaged the land, capturing the men, women and children who were exiled into Babylon. Everything they had built, worked for and developed, was destroyed. Everything they loved was taken from them, they no longer had free will or freedom of speech, they were prisoners in a foreign land. They were whipped, beaten and tortured, the men were castrated, the women raped. I'm not sure life could have gotten any worse for them.

Judah was known for it's music and worship to God and the Babylonian masters would mock their captives and taunt them to sing the sacred songs they used in worship to God in the temple. Psalm 137 is a record of this:

"Beside the rivers of Babylon, we sat and wept as we thought of Jerusalem. We put away our harps, hanging them on the branches of poplar trees. For our captors demanded a song from us. Our tormentors insisted on a joyful hymn: "Sing us one of those songs of Jerusalem!" But how can we sing the songs of the LORD while in a pagan land?"
Psalm 137:1-4
~ (NLT) New Living Translation ~

You may not be in Babylon today, but you may still feel like you're in captivity, feeling trapped by your problems, enslaved by a situation that feels beyond your control.

Just like the enemy took the people of Judah into exile and taunted them, you may feel like your enemy, the devil, is taunting you today, asking you "where is your God now?"

See if you can sing in the midst of a broken marriage!

The enemy is goading you, **try and sing to God during the family crisis!** He's taunting you, **try praising your God when you've received a bad health report.**

For the enemy knows that if he can silence you, he disarms you **for your song is your weapon of warfare and your victory shout.**

He's mocking you, to humiliate you, so that you will remain silent because he knows worship is a choice and not a feeling.

And if you open your mouth to God in this season, no matter how difficult; when your frequency aligns with His, it will radically change the atmosphere over your life.

The people of Judah were mistaken. They presumed that they could not worship God because of their location. They asked, '*How can we sing the LORD'S song in a strange and foreign land*?' In other words, they weren't in *Zion* (Jerusalem). They weren't in the temple of God (which had been destroyed by the Babylonians). They didn't know that they could praise God wherever they were and that He would hear them.

Do not let the enemy deceive you into thinking that just because your life is not where you think it ought to be, you can't sing. Worship is about a *person*, not a place, and the person is **JESUS**.

The New Testament records a story

in the book of Acts. Paul and Silas sang praises to God after they had been whipped and beaten, bound with chains and thrown into prison. They understood they did not need to be in a church building or even in a good situation to get tuned in to the same frequency as God.

When we worship from a difficult place, a sound goes up before Heaven and God hears our sacrificial worship. You're not singing because you feel like it. You're not worshipping because it's Sunday. It is the cry of your spirit longing to connect with your God.

"About midnight Paul and Silas were praying and singing hymns to God, and the other prisoners were listening to them. Suddenly there was such a violent earthquake that the foundations of the prison were shaken. At once all the prison doors flew open, and everyone's chains came loose."
Acts 16:25-26
~ (NIV: New International Version) ~

It was not only Paul and Silas's chains that came loose, but also everyone else who was being held prisoner – their chains fell off too. Because worship had altered the atmosphere, it made way for the power of God to move.

PRAYER FOR TODAY

Lord God, thank you that you will never leave me or forsake me. Your presence is not dependent on my situation and no matter where I find myself in life, I can tune in to your frequency and be in communion with you. I ask for the power of your Holy Spirit to help me not to ride the waves of my emotions, but to be mindful that when I choose to open up my mouth in times of uncertainty, miracles can happen.

DAY EIGHTEEN
HEAR ME ROAR

> *"Stay alert! Watch out for your great enemy, the devil. He prowls around like a roaring lion, looking for someone to devour."*
> *1 Peter 5:8*
> *(NLT: New Living Translation)*

HOW TO SPEAK BRAVE

We can read scriptures like this and almost feel like a sitting duck waiting to be devoured! But this scripture was not written to intimidate you. It was written to encourage you to live your life prepared. So let us not become complacent or neglect the fact that there is a war taking place for your soul, and the enemy is prowling around like a hungry lion ready to pounce on his prey.

If you've ever watched any nature documentaries, like the BBC's *Planet Earth* TV series with David Attenborough, or the *National Geographic Wild* (Nat Geo Wild) TV channel, you will have seen animals that often become the lion's lunch. It tends to be that one animal that has become distracted or separated from the herd. Perhaps it was doing its everyday ordinary things – head down, eating grass or lapping water, not being alert – when suddenly, out of nowhere, its world is turned into chaos.

We all know what it's like to have the enemy suddenly descend into our world:
- The doctors report you never saw coming
- The relational breakdown you never thought would happen to you
- The redundancy
- The rejection

These are all things that can *appear suddenly* and blindside you. Let me show you in a very practical way what this looks like and how we can deal with the enemy. You may remember on Day 9, we looked at *'what's in your hand'* and I mentioned Jael and her tent peg. Well, we're going to get to know her a little better today.

We first meet Jael in **Judges 4:17-19**. For her, it was a day just like any other. She was going about her business, tending to her home (a tent), peeling potatoes, baking bread, sweeping the floor, when suddenly, the Israelites' number 1 enemy bursts in. His name is Sisera, and he is the commander of the Canaanite army.

Israel was at that very moment, at war with Canaan. Only Sisera had escaped the battle on foot and ran to the place of the tent dwellers for covering. He threw himself through the canvas flaps of Jael's tent and demanded that she hide him.

> *"I'm thirsty," he said. "Please give me some water." She opened a skin of milk, gave him a drink, and covered him up. "Stand in the doorway of the tent," he told her. "If someone comes by and asks you, 'Is anyone in there?' say 'No.' "*
> *~ Judges 4:19-20 (NIV: New International Version) ~*

The enemy of her people has just landed *suddenly* in her home and is essentially saying to her, "hide me and lie for me."

'Stand by the door of the tent and if anyone comes looking for me, tell them, there's no one here' he says, and then he settled down undercover in the background of her home.

The tactics of the enemy have not changed. Today he wants to turn up in your world, unannounced and uninvited, to lay low, in secret, in the background of your life, whispering lies to you. He wants you to stand at the door of your life (so to speak), and when someone comes by, he wants you to put on a fake smile and lie.

- When someone compliments you – he'll tell you you're not worth it.
- When they speak of your success – he'll remind you of your failures.
- When they love on you – he'll tell you it's not real, that you're going to be rejected.
- Whatever truth they speak – he'll reject it with a lie.

The enemy knows if he can influence the woman and get her to believe his lies, then she will go on to influence many others. She will get into her husband's ear. She will bend the mind of her children.

She will gather girlfriends and spread the enemy's words, his lies, and the insecurity and chaos they create, will be like a deadly disease.

But God makes it very clear in His Word how we are to handle this:

"And do not give the devil an opportunity [to lead you into sin by holding a grudge, or nurturing anger, or harboring resentment, or cultivating bitterness]."
~ Ephesians 4:27 (AMP: Amplified Bible) ~

So when the devil springs himself on you, and begins to make his bed in your home and whispers lies into your ear, we need to follow Jael's example.

Something rose up on the inside of her, a defiance against the enemy. I can imagine her telling herself, *'This is my home! This is my family! This isn't right!'*

Now don't get me wrong, Jael was no superhero. She wasn't a leader, a teacher or a great influencer. Jael was probably a stay-at-home mum. She kept her tent in order. Only, on this day something was very out of order, and she found the courage and the strength to put that wrong thing right.

Your home is your territory. Your house is your responsibility. The threshold of your tent – is the front door into your life – that's your boundary line. You get to say who deserves to be allowed in. You don't have to be a person of title, position or prominence to take authority in the areas of your life that the enemy is trying to move in on. God has given you a clear instruction to obey, *'give no opportunity to the devil'* and *'do not give the devil a foothold.'*

Sisera was so sure of himself hiding in Jael's tent that he even went to sleep! He totally underestimated the strength of this everyday housewife. Brace yourself, what happens next is a bit gruesome.

'But Jael, Heber's wife, picked up a tent peg and a hammer and went quietly to him [Sisera] while he lay fast asleep, exhausted. She drove the peg through his temple into the ground, and he died.' That's right. Jael took a tent peg and a mallet and drove it through his skull!

Jael's name in Hebrew means '*value*' this woman wanted to protect what was of most value to her – her family and her home.

If you could only recognise how valuable you are to God, then you too can find the courage to drive out the enemy who's been lying in wait and oppressing you for years.

You may fear the roar of the enemy, but there is a roar that the enemy fears even more, a sound that is greater and more powerful, a sound that makes the enemy tremble, a roar he knows he can't compete with – it's the sound of the daughters of God awakening!

It wasn't just what Jael did physically with the tent peg that took the enemy out that day; it was the sound she released from her spirit, it was the sound of a decision, it was the sound of determination, a roar of courage from her innermost being as she ploughed that mallet down.

The devil fears that sound most of all, for he knows that there's a lioness inside of us that just woke up, and our roar has the backing of Heaven and it's King.

So girlfriend, take back what the devil is trying to take from you. Tell yourself the truth. Don't entertain negativity. Deal with the lie harshly, know your worth, declare your value, speak to that situation – You are a lioness, feminine to the core. Now open up your mouth and let the enemy HEAR YOU ROAR!

PRAYER FOR TODAY
Lord, forgive me for the times when I have been complacent. Please show me the areas of my life where I have allowed the enemy to come in and make himself at home. You have given me the responsibility to guard and govern what is mine. Please give me the courage to stand up for the truth, to put an end to the deceit of the enemy's lies and to take back what he has stolen. I remind myself daily that if my God is for me, then nothing can stand against me, and I do not need to fear. Amen.

DAY NINETEEN
HOLD ON TO YOUR DREAM

"Forget the former things, do not dwell on the past. See, I am doing a new thing! Now it springs up, do you not perceive it? I am making a way in the wilderness and streams in the wasteland."
Isaiah 43:18-19
(NIV: New International Version)

HOW TO SPEAK BRAVE
A New York Times article suggests that '*Learning becomes more difficult as we age not because we have trouble absorbing new information, but because we fail to forget the old stuff.*'

We moved house as a family a few years ago, and because our new home wasn't ready yet we had to put our furniture and belongings into storage. I took everything! My husband, Luke, would repeatedly ask me, "are you sure you want to keep all of this?" I kept hold of everything. I remember how hard we had saved for certain things. There were sentimental things that had been passed down through the family. Things we had kept from our first year of marriage.

Well, what we thought would be six weeks of storage turned into six months! When we finally emptied the storage unit to move into our new home I realised that I no longer required or wanted at least half of the stuff that we had stored.

As we brought the old furniture into our new home I realised how tired it looked. Fashion had changed. My taste had changed and the old stuff just didn't seem to fit our new house. Luke raised his eyebrows as he looked at me and said, "we've paid a high price to hold onto stuff we no longer need."

Do you know that spiritually speaking we can do the same? We have old mindsets and memories that we're not ready to let go of. We have habits and ways, language and speech, that suited our old life but they don't fit the new life we're now living. When we made the decision to follow

Christ, He was giving us the opportunity for a fresh start.

2 Corinthians 5:17 says, "***Therefore, if anyone is in Christ, he is a new creation. The old has passed away; behold, the new has come***."

In the same way that my new home could not facilitate both the old furniture and the new furniture, I had to decide to get rid of some old stuff to make room for new. We have to do likewise with our thought-life.

According to that New York Times article, we have trouble absorbing new in formation because we can't let go of the old stuff. They did a study involving genetically modified mice and found that *'as the modified mice entered adulthood, they were less capable of weakening connections that already existed, and that made it hard for them to form robust new long-term memories.*

Think of it as writing on a blank piece of white paper versus a newspaper page. If there's already writing on the newspaper page, it's hard to write new memories over the top. If we hold on to the past, it's hard to write a new future.

The mind has a capacity. By not letting go of old ways, then we can cap our capacity.

Let me give you some examples:

- You will never see the new thing God is doing in your life – whilst holding on to what has been.
- You will never believe anything can go right for you – if you're still talking about the stuff that went wrong.
- You will never see yourself as an achiever – whilst you're telling everyone about your loss or past failures.
- You will never move on relationally – whilst still talking about the divorce or your ex.
- You will never receive healing – if you keep reminding yourself and others of how badly you were hurt.

How do we ever move forward in life when we carry so many wounds from the past?

Some people never move forward, they remain stuck.

Negative past experiences can hurt you emotionally, damage you psychologically and scar your memory, leaving you broken and bitter and saying things like:

- I will never get married or be in a relationship again.
- I will never trust again.
- I will never be part of a church again.
- I will never let someone get close enough to hurt me again.

When God says, '*See, I am doing a new thing*!' I imagine Him saying to us, "*get a new perspective*!"

Do you know God wants you to create new memories? It might seem strange because surely a memory comes from an experience of the past, and you can't change the past, right?

Think of it like this: if your previous experiences of relationships or marriage, physical health or employment, finances or friendships, have not been positive ones, the past may not change, but your perspective and interpretation of the past can change!

I don't think God wants us to dwell on the past. I think He's saying, "do not allow an old memory to keep you from living your best life!"

> **"Don't copy the behavior and customs of this world, but let God transform you into a new person by changing the way you think. Then you will learn to know God's will for you, which is good and pleasing and perfect."**
> *~ Romans 12:2 (NLT: New Living Translation) ~*

So how do we renew our mind? We do this by '*taking captive every thought to make it obedient to Christ*.' We clear out the old thoughts and replace them with new ones. We let go of the old ways of thinking and take in some new information. We find out what God says about our situation through His Word, rather than what our past experiences tell us.

- What does God say about marriage? Not what my ex says about it! Not what the world or Hollywood movies say about it!
- What does God say about me? Not what the people around me call me. Not what my star sign tells me!

It's all here in this book called the living Word of God! The Bible is as alive and relevant today as it was thousands of years ago when it was first written. Through its pages, God wants to renew our minds (alter our thinking) to set us up strong for a better future. As we learn from scripture, it changes our perspective and how we see things, helping us to let go of the past and form new memories.

- Hope replaces hopelessness
- Joy overcomes sorrow
- Faith begins to grow where fear once thrived

However, if we don't know what the Bible says, how can we counteract our old thoughts with new ones? Let's be honest, it's a pretty big book with a lot of text to memorise for those of us who can't even remember our PIN number! (Hello friend!)

Researchers at the University of Edinburgh have studied the relationship between music and memory. They found that singing was a great way to help with learning, for example, a new language. In the experiment, they split 60 adults into one of three "listen-and-repeat" learning groups: speaking, rhythmic or singing, and taught them to learn phrases in an unfamiliar language. They chose Hungarian as it is a difficult language to master, completely different in structure and sound system from English. After the 15-minute learning period, the singers came out on top in most of the tests.

According to the authors, this is the first time that research has produced experimental evidence that singing can help with learning another language. For many of us, reading the Word of God can often feel like a foreign language. No sooner do you get to the end of one chapter, than you can hardly remember what you read at the beginning of it.

RAISE A
HALLELUJAH

However, when we praise and worship God, the songs we sing are the Word of God put to music with lyrics inspired from the Bible. You will often find that what you sang in church on Sunday, you're still humming at your desk on Wednesday. Why? Because you're singing scripture. When you get an understanding of the power of God behind the words you are singing, it is life-changing.

So, sing sister! Whether you can hold a tune or not, whether you feel like it or not, whether it is a good day or not a good day, God's power is released into your situation when you open your mouth and sing his Word back to Him.

Singing, according to the Bible, is not a suggestion or an emotion – it is a command.

"Let the word of Christ dwell in you richly, teaching and admonishing one another in all wisdom, singing psalms and hymns and spiritual songs, with thankfulness in your hearts to God."
~ Colossians 3:16 (ESV: English Standard Version) ~

"And do not get drunk with wine, for that is debauchery, but be filled with the Spirit, addressing one another in psalms and hymns and spiritual songs, singing and making melody to the Lord with your heart, giving thanksalways and for everything to God the Father in the name of our Lord Jesus Christ."
~ Ephesians 5:18-20 (ESV: English Standard Version) ~

So your singing is right up there on God's priority list!

Singing is what you should do, especially when you know that there is nothing else that you can do.

When you are facing an impossible situation, find a song that reminds you of the goodness and the faithfulness of God. There will be a rising of hope in your heart, and a confident assurance that He has got this.

PRAYER FOR TODAY
Lord, may I always make more room for you by shifting some of my wrong thinking and focusing on your word. Your word is life-giving, bringing hope and healing. I need it in my life, I need it for my future, and I need it for my peace of mind. May I find a song rising in my heart daily that brings glory to your name and in doing so, may my life be changed so that I will never be the same again. Amen.

DAY TWENTY
THE POWER IS IN YOUR MOUTH

"I will praise the LORD at all times. I will constantly speak His praises."
Psalm 34:1 (NLT: New Living Translation)

HOW TO SPEAK BRAVE

Notice that the psalmist writes that he will praise the Lord at *all times*. That's a bold statement, right? It's easy to praise God when life is good and everything seems to be on our side. But when a crisis hits or a problem arises, we can barely break a smile and we feel we have nothing to praise God for. Well, that's what the enemy wants you to believe because he understands something that many of us fail to realise – that praise is a spiritual weapon that we can use against him!

James 4:7 teaches us that when we resist the enemy he flees from us. So how do we resist the enemy? By turning our attention towards God. The best way that we can do that is in praise and worship. Since God inhabits our praises, the enemy cannot be present at the same time. Darkness and light do not cohabit. Therefore when you make a conscious decision to praise God despite your circumstances you are making way for your miracle.

The story of the Israelites coming out of slavery in Egypt and making their way towards the promised land often reads like a fairy tale. I remember as a child the images that we were shown at Sunday school of children skipping and men laughing as they crossed over the Red Sea on dry land, pictures of the waters banked up on either side of them as the people led their cattle across the dry sea bed.

But children's stories often soften the harsh reality that really took place.

In **Exodus 12:31**, we read how the Israelites made their escape from Egypt. The Israelites were being pursued by the Egyptian army, the enemy that had held them in captivity for 430 years. To me, this sounds like a frantic hurry across the seabed, terrified for their lives, not the cheerful scenes from my childhood picture books.

Nobody knows for sure how many Israelites there were, with estimates ranging from 30,000 to 2 million people. The Bible account suggests *'there were about six hundred thousand men on foot, besides women and children. Many other people went up with them, and also large droves of livestock, both flocks and herds.'* We don't know exactly where the Red Sea crossing occurred, but if it were a mile wide at the crossing point, some people have calculated that it might have taken 3 or 4 hours for all the Israelites to cross over.

Now picture this moment as if you were making the journey yourself.

You've just lost your home. In a single night, you've been told to pack up all your belongings. But there's no removal van. You've got to somehow get your flocks and cattle to travel with you (whilst you're fleeing for your life). Your dough pot (bread maker) is tied to the clothes around your shoulders, and you can only take what you are able to carry – oh, and there were no suitcases! You might have a few screaming children in tow, maybe even a baby, or you might be 9 months pregnant and going into labour! Maybe you have elderly family members. Perhaps there's someone in your family unit with a disability or illness. Escaping on foot with very little preparation or help would have felt overwhelming.

Imagine all those people and animals, running for their lives. If someone falls, they could get trampled over. There would have been parents looking for missing children, elderly people stumbling over rocks, everyone screaming and shouting out for different family members, the fear that the enemy was getting closer. So they are frantically rushing across the Red Sea – bedraggled, bruised and broken, ripped clothes, sprained ankles, grazed knees – between two walls of water, crossing over on the miraculously dry ground.

Imagine how they must have felt on the other side of the waters, hours later, exhausted but alive!

But this is what I want you to see, the most astonishing thing happened when they were at their lowest ebb, in their weakest moment, afraid for their lives, facing an impossible situation.

"Then Moses and the Israelites sang this song to the Lord: "I will sing to the Lord, for he is highly exalted. Both horse and driver he has hurled into the sea. "The Lord is my strength and my defense; he has become my salvation. He is my God, and I will praise him, my father's God, and I will exalt him."
~ Exodus 15:1-2 (NIV: New International Version) ~

Their song was not out of feeling, they had lost everything!

That song was a war cry, a sign to the enemy, that though you've pushed me, though you've tested me, though you've taken everything from me, my war cry is praise and in that praise my father hears me. I am declaring my future, I'm taking back what you've stolen from me, I'm dancing on a new day, I'm singing in my spirit, because on the inside I can see what is not yet showing up on the outside.

That which you meant to destroy my life with, my God will take those broken remnants and rebuild me, and I will be fit for His glory, because this is not my end it's just a chapter in my story.

Girlfriend, when you feel at your lowest, that is the time your praise should be at its highest because your voice lets the enemy know that you are not done yet. Open your mouth and declare *'I have a future to possess, a relationship to rebuild, a home to purchase, a friend to forgive, a child to raise, people to love and a lot of life worth living.'* So, find your voice and remind the enemy that though he bruised your heel with the (divorce, diagnosis, rejection or abuse), when you open your mouth, you will crush his head. For if your God is for you then who or what could ever be against you?

PRAYER FOR TODAY
Lord, help me to remember that when I am weak, you are strong. When I'm at my lowest, you want to show me your greatest. When I'm hurting, you want to hold me. When I'm broken, you want to heal me. You are a good, good father. So may I never withhold my praise to you. Help me to be mindful that praise is not a feeling but a decision I make based on who you are, not how I am. And when I raise my praise, the enemy is silenced. I love you, Jesus. Amen.

PART THREE

HOW TO REMAIN BRAVE

DAY TWENTY-ONE
THE COUNTERFEIT LIFE

"The thief comes only to steal and kill and destroy; I have come that they may have life, and have it to the full."
John 10:10 (NIV: New International Version)

HOW TO REMAIN BRAVE

Did you know that God has a pre-destined (pre-chosen) life for you, a life of blessing and abundance, with the intention of seeing you win and succeed? A life of longevity, prosperity and good health. That is God's preferred (chosen) plan for us. But we live in a fallen world where life can often feel far removed from the designed plans that He has for us.

The book of Genesis, describes in detail Eve's epic fail when she ate of the forbidden fruit. Eve was the first woman in the whole of humanity and she didn't set the sisterhood up strong at all.

I'm sure that if we get the chance to meet up with her in Heaven, she's going to have a lot of questions from a lot of frustrated women, who just want to know: *"Girl, what was your problem? Why couldn't you just stick to the rest of the orchard? You know, all the trees you were allowed to eat! Why did you have to bite the one thing that you were forbidden to have? Because the rest of us have been paying the price for it ever since!"*

So often we read this story with the mindset, *'If I was Eve, I wouldn't have been so foolish. If I was Eve, I would have been smarter and wiser.'*

But, truth be told, we all have an *'Eve'* on the inside of us and every single day we are presented with an *'Eve-type situation.'* Most days we fail too.

How many times have you made a choice or a decision and the very next day you find yourself reflecting on yesterday and *'kicking your own backside'* with thoughts like *'why did I do that! How could I have been so foolish.'* Well, you did it for the very same reason as Eve – you fell victim to the enemy's deception.

Genesis 3 tells us that the serpent was the shrewdest (craftiest) of all the animals God had ever made. He was clever, cunning and deceptive. In his conversation with Eve, he told her a lie but gift-wrapped it as the truth.

She may have bitten into the forbidden fruit, but it was the lie that she swallowed first and that lie stole her identity, killed her innocence and destroyed her future. Eve fell victim to Satan's sales pitch. His words were convincing – "Did God *really* say, 'You must not eat from any tree in the garden'?"

> *"For God knows that when you eat from it your eyes*
> *will be opened, and you will be like God, knowing good and evil."*
> *~ Genesis 3:5 (NIV: New International Version) ~*

Though I find Eve's disobedience frustrating, there is a far greater tragedy than just her moment of weakness. It was the realisation that Eve had forgotten who she really was for she was already like God, she was made in His image. [Genesis 1:26]

Here we see that the deception gives way to confusion. Satan had convinced Eve that she was flawed and lacking. He deceived her into believing that life's fulfilment would come from something external. He persuaded her to cross the boundary that her Heavenly father had set in place to protect her. In the New Testament, Satan is referred to as 'the father of lies.' The way he interacts with women today is no different to his encounter with Eve in the Garden of Eden. He lies to you, deceives you and takes from you the good that God has intended for you.

He will have you believe that right is wrong and wrong is right. He sows discord, breeds jealousy and he will destroy your integrity until you begin to forget whose image and likeness you were made in. You will listen to gossip and believe every negative word spoken over you. You'll take on board every low-level comment made about you. You will strive to find or manufacture the perfect life, trying to live up to the standards and expectations of others and be forever searching for peace and purpose. All the while, you would be desperately trying to become who you were already created to be.

You see how easy it is? When you lend an ear to words that are not edifying, uplifting or encouraging, when you listen to a lie, deception opens a door and invites in confusion. You forget who you truly are and whose image you were created in – and whose daughter you are - a child of God.

The word '**counterfeit**' means: *made to be an exact imitation of something with the intention to deceive or defraud*. The dictionary definition gives us the best language to describe the enemy's intentions. His sole purpose is to take your promised life and replace it with a counterfeit life that makes you believe it's the same, but it's not.

My son loves a breakfast cereal called 'KRAVE', a bowl full of sugary chocolate pillows, probably given that name because of its addictive taste! However, I have discovered that a certain supermarket has created its own brand of cereal, a counterfeit version. It looks almost identical – a similar shape, colour and size, a similar box (but much cheaper!) – these are called 'KRAZE.' They just had one letter change! I bought them hoping my son wouldn't notice. But I was wrong! He said, "Mum, once you've tasted the real thing, nothing else comes close!"

Girls, this is your reminder, nothing else comes close to having a real relationship with God. Nothing compares to the life that God has destined for you. Nothing compares to the plans He has for your relationships, welfare, finances, career and much more.

Don't fall for the lie that says the Bible is old, dated and boring. Don't listen to the world's advice, that you should lower your standards, lift your boundaries and abandon your morals, on a promise that '*you'll have way more fun!*'. Don't fall for the lie and spend your years living in a counterfeit culture. The Word of God is the breath of God. It is life-giving and following its wisdom will take your life above and beyond your wildest expectations.

PRAYER FOR TODAY
Heavenly Father, may I seek you daily as you reveal to me the plan you have for my life and the purpose I was born for. I pray that I may cleave to you and your ways and as I do, may I know that my life will flourish and prosper. Amen.

DAY TWENTY-TWO
DELAYS, DETOURS AND DESTINY

"Trust in the Lord with all your heart, And lean not on your own understanding; In all your ways acknowledge Him, and He shall direct your paths."
Proverbs 3:5-6
(NKJV: New King James Version)

HOW TO REMAIN BRAVE

I don't know if you're anything like me, but I hate being stuck in roadworks! Facing a roadblock or being sent on a diversion leaves me frustrated!

Not so long ago I was driving into our home city to meet my husband for lunch and I got stuck! I sat on the main road for forty minutes watching the diggers and trucks demolishing and repairing the street in front of me. There were barricades to stop me from going forward and diversion signs to re-route my journey. Everything was moving so much more slowly than I needed it to.

But as I sat there feeling rather disgruntled, watching time pass by, I gave myself a pep-talk, reminding myself that roadworks are necessary. There are only ever roadblocks or diversions when something us under construction or demolition, being built up or torn

down. Roadblocks are necessary to make travel safe.

I began to think about how this relates to our faith life. How often en route to our destination do we come up against a roadblock, an unexpected problem, a health problem, a difficult relational situation, bad news, or a negative report. At times it can feel so frustrating because none of us have ever scheduled time in our diaries for a problem.

However, have you considered that the delay to your dream, the diversion to your destination or the roadblock problem you are facing today could be a God-made obstruction, rather than a dead-end situation? Could it be for a reason? You see, when it comes to dreams and goals, we are always interested in getting there fast. But God is more concerned with getting you there right. He knows that there is something just as bad as not getting to your destination and that's getting you there *unprepared*.

Unprepared means you're unequipped, underskilled, and so though you might reach your goal, fulfil your dream or arrive at your destination but you can't enjoy it. You have what you wanted, but you can't appreciate it. You're living the dream, yet it feels like a nightmare.

Imagine going on holiday and forgetting your suitcase: you would be at the right destination but completely unprepared for it. Imagine getting the job, but not having the skills or management needed to handle the pressure.

So, to prepare us for when we finally arrive at our purpose, dreams and goals in life, God may purposefully put a roadblock in your life that will cause you to stop. This could be a diversion to re-route your life from where it was going, slowing down your journey. Why? Because He's got some work to do on you, preparing something better for you, constructing something within you, so that you'll be ready for the new. That's going to take a bit of time.

So while He's working on you, He'll take you the long way around.

Maybe He's wanting to dig out some things to reconstruct you and restore you, like old mindsets, wrong habits, or unhealthy relationships.

Maybe He wants to repair some things that are broken, like your confidence, your trust, or your faith.

He will allow a detour or a delay whilst He works on getting you ready for the future you've been praying for.

I mentioned that I was going to meet my husband for lunch. Well, I was going there intending to have one of those 'wife-to-husband chats.' You know the type I mean? The kind of conversation where I've got a lot to say and he needs to listen!

(Every wife knows what I'm talking about!) Well, do you know, in the time it took me to go the long way around, having re-routed, and by the time I got to the restaurant I had reconsidered how I wanted to say what I wanted to say! My mood and attitude had changed. My tone was different. My heart had softened, and we had a lovely afternoon of constructive and fruitful conversation.

I'm so glad it took me longer to get to where I needed to be because, by the time I got there, I was right in my spirit and emotions.

If you feel like you're up against another roadblock in your life, if you feel like you're on a never-ending diversion trying to move nearer towards your dreams or goals, instead of lettingfrustration eat away at you, be at peace knowing God is doing a work within you.

Ask Him to show you what He's working on within you. You will get there my friend, but it will be in His timing, not yours. His strength and not your own. And when you do arrive at your desired destination, whether it's the friendship you've always dreamt about, a family, marriage partner, date, job, promotion or pay rise, you'll be prepared for it and flourish in it.

PRAYER FOR TODAY
Lord, we live in a world of fast and immediate expectations. We want it all now and we don't like to wait for anything. But today I choose to have a different spirit about me. Though Imay not understand the reasons why I have to go through what I go through, I trust in a God whom I know will get me through. I submit myself to your construction, giving you permission to tear down and build up my life as you see fit, and lovingly repair that which has been damaged or broken. I want to be ready for all that you have in store for me. Amen.

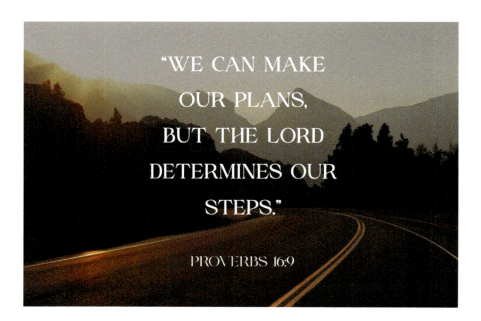

DAY TWENTY-THREE
CHOOSE YOUR VIEW

"Your eyes are a window for your body. When they are good, you have all the light you need."
Matthew 6:22
(CEV: Contemporary English Version)

HOW TO REMAIN BRAVE

Think about your house for a moment. Though it is one building it has many windows. The view you see depends on which window you're looking out from. The front window may look onto your driveway or out across the street. Perhaps the rear window reveals a garden, trees, plants and a shed. The same house has many windows, each one giving you a very different perspective.

Some windows may have a stunning view. Perhaps you've got a favourite spot to look out from, an open window to gaze through or let the fresh air and sunshine in. But there are also windows in our homes that remain shut, covered over, perhaps with frosted glass or an opaque finish to hide a view that's not so great. It could be facing a wall or a next-door neighbour's gable end.

Our scripture today describes your eyes as *'a window for your body'* ('our eyes are the window to the soul).

Therefore, what you fix your focus on matters. What you look at has a direct effect on who you become and what you will do with your life. I've heard it said that *'what we see with our eyes shows up in our lives'*.

So, what are you looking at? What is the algorithm that populates your social media feed? What is your most chosen type of Netflix movie? Who do you hang out with? What do you read? What do you watch on your screens? What information are you taking in? Because whatever you spend time looking at today is shaping who you will become tomorrow.

Did you know that your mood is influenced by what you see? Think about it. The type of movie you watch has a direct effect on how you feel. If you watch a thriller, you can feel anxious, to the point were you don't even want to go to the bathroom, in case the crazy guy is hiding behind the shower curtain – even though you don't even have a shower curtain! But because you've seen what happens on the movie, you're scared it might happen to you too!

Not every window in your house has to be opened. If the view isn't good, the neighbours are problematic, or the weather is bad, then you make a clear choice to keep your window closed or covered because you don't want what is on the outside to infiltrate the inside. Well, likewise, you too have a choice where to fix your focus, what you allow the windows of your soul to be opened to.

You decide what is wholesome to watch. You get to choose what you engage with on social media. You select the friends you spend time with and the relationships you build because what you see influences who you become.

So be mindful today to protect your thoughts, feelings and emotions by choosing what and who you give your time and attention to. You can choose to close your laptop down. You can choose to ignore your phone. You can decide not to use social media. You can delete, mute, unfollow, block. There is a lot that you can control because you have been given free will and the power to choose.

So make this the day when you allow the light of God to flood into every area of your life, body, mind, soul and spirit by dwelling and looking at whatever is good.

"Whatever is true, whatever is noble, whatever is right, whatever is pure, whatever is lovely, whatever is admirable—if anything is excellent or praiseworthy—think about such things."
~ Philippians 4:8 (NIV: New International Version) ~

PRAYER FOR TODAY
Lord, today I ask for supernatural strength from you as I fix my eyes on you and look for your goodness, your kindness and your beauty in the world around me. Fill me with your revelation light so that when night falls I may sleep easily and rest well. Amen.

DAY TWENTY-FOUR
TAKE A SEAT AT THE TABLE

HOW TO REMAIN BRAVE

I love dinner parties! I love going to them and I love hosting them. I'm not the best cook in the world but I take great pleasure in preparing the table. When I invite friends over for dinner it's always with a purpose, even if it's simply to share the enjoyment of their company.

At my table, everyone has a place with a name setting, and I take great delight in the detail. Flowers, candles and decorations adorn my table in the hope that my family and friends feel valued and loved.

There is a heartfelt story in **2 Samuel 9** about an invitation to King David's table. We are introduced to a man called Mephibosheth who was the son of Jonathan and the grandson of the previous king, Saul. When he was a small child, the place where he lived was attacked and all his immediate and extended family were killed. Mephibosheth was five years old when this happened and his nurse maid picked him up in her arms and fled into the night to save his life.

> *"You prepare a table before me in the presence of my enemies..."*
> *Psalm 23:5*
> *(NIV: New International Version)*

As she ran she slipped and dropped him and both his legs were broken.

Mephibosheth was left lame. Unable to walk, unable to work, unable to have any quality of life whatsoever - he would have been treated as a social outcast. As a grown man, he made his home in a place called Lo Debar. Some Bible scholars think that Lo Debar means 'no pasture' or 'no thing'... essentially, it was Nothing Town. A remote village with nothing really going for it. It was a desolate place, a place of barrenness and poverty. Nothing good ever happened in Lo Debar. Following King Saul's death, David has now become king over all of Israel. He has managed to subdue and conquer many of the neighbouring nations – the Philistines, the Moabites, the Edomites, Ammonites and Amalekites. One day David is reminiscing over the goodness of God in his own life and remembering his good friend Jonathan.

It prompts him to ask the question, "Is there anyone still left of the house of Saul to whom I can show kindness for Jonathan's sake?" In other words, is there anyone of Jonathan's family who survived the attack from years ago.

The story goes on to tell how a servent came forth and began to speak about a man who had been found in Lo Debar whom it was rumoured about to be a relative of King Saul. And so the servant is brought before King David. That is when David learns the story of Mephibosheth, the last remaining son of Jonathan.

The Bible doesn't exactly explain how Mephibosheth came to be brought to King David's palace, but I like to imagine the scene like this: a search party goes out from Jerusalem to Lo Debar, a remote village in the middle of nowhere, a town called '*Nothing*'.

They go into the slums looking for a crippled man. Perhaps he hasn't washed or shaved. Perhaps he is dressed in rags. Perhaps when the king's servants arrive he is frightened for his life – what could King David possibly want with *me*? Here's what happens next:

> *"Don't be afraid," David said to him, "for I will surely show you kindness for the sake of your father Jonathan. I will restore to you all the land that belonged to your grandfather Saul, and you will always eat at my table." Mephibosheth bowed down and said, "What is your servant, that you should notice a dead dog like me?"*
> *~ 2 Samuel 9: 7-8 (NIV) New International Version ~*

This gives us a glimpse into how Mephibosheth saw himself. His self-esteem was at rock bottom. He had nothing to live for and nothing to look forward to. It wasn't just his legs that were broken, he was also broken on the inside from all the years of suffering.

And yet, King David raises him up, gives him honour and invites him to sit at his table like family. He is adopted into the king's family, eating with David, just like his own sons. Seated at the table he would eat the royal food and drink the finest wine and engage in conversation with the king. The king would remind him of who he really was, that he has royal blood flowing through his veins and that what had happened to him should not be allowed to define him. When seated at the king's table, Mephibosheth's deformity and disability would have been covered. For the first time he was face to face with others instead of being looked down on. He would have been spoken to with kindness and respect and would have been accepted as a man instead of rejected as someone who is less than.

The table covered his legs, the memory of what had been, the shame of his condition, and the pain of his past.

This story is a true reflection of God's love towards you.

There is an invitation for you to sit at the table of the King of Kings daily. A place where you are loved, accepted and valued, regardless of the story surrounding your past, despite the mistakes you've made or the hurt that's been caused to you.

Precious girlfriend, today God has set a table for you to be seated in His company, and it's an extravagant spread, an over-the-top banquet. Kindness covers it, goodness flows from it, blessings are the bountiful centre-piece, and grace and mercy are served up on it.

You are His guest of honour, and when you take time to sit in His presence and allow yourself to be nourished and fed by his word, you will see how shame falls off you. Darkness leaves you, depression lifts from you and you will feel satisfied and loved beyond measure. So today, why don't you take a seat? He's waiting for your company.

PRAYER FOR TODAY
God, I thank you that you don't look at my mess or my past mistakes, but you look at me from across your table with eyes of love and forgiveness. Help me to accept that I have the right to be here because I'm seated at your invitation. Today I choose to feast on your goodness, kindness, love and mercy. Though I cannot change anything about my past, your grace covers it and for that, I am forever thankful. Amen.

DAY TWENTY-FIVE
WHAT YOU WEAR MATTERS

"She makes coverings for her bed; she is clothed in fine linen and purple."
Proverbs 31:22
(NIV: New International Version)

HOW TO REMAIN BRAVE

Proverbs 31 is all about a woman of noble character. You may wonder why this scripture about her character talks so much about her clothing. How is what she's wearing relevant to who she is and who she's becoming, you might ask?

Well, did you know that you can please or displease the Lord according to what you choose to dress in, metaphorically speaking? Now you might be thinking, 'how do I know which outfit would please the Lord? Is he offended when I pray in my dressing gown?' I mean, the mind boggles when you think about this literally.

The truth is that clothes are mentioned throughout the Bible because the clothing people wore was quite significant in biblical times and represented much more than our outfit choices do today.

In Biblical culture, your clothes said a lot about who you were. They represented your level of education, status, position, title or rank, i.e. the pecking order of society was made known through the clothes that you wore. Kings wore royal robes, while beggars and those who were lame or maimed wore a type of cloak and sash and the colour of their sash indicated their disability. Clothes of uncomfortable coarse material were worn during times of grief or repentance. Prostitutes dressed a certain way so that they could be recognised by their clothing and leather belts were worn as a sign of poverty.

In our scripture today, the *Proverbs 31 woman* wears fine linen and purple, a colour of royalty and high status. Bible scholars believe that the colour purple carried with it a great deal of nobility and prestige. It was one of the most expensive dyes known to the ancient eastern culture. One process to get a dye called *Tyrian purple* involved thousands of marine snail shells that had been boiled for days! The linen would then have to be dipped twice to get the rich purple colour.

You can see why purple was only worn by royalty or high-ranking officials. It was a symbol of wealth and prosperity because only this calibre of people could afford it.

If there was so much meaning and symbolism in the physical clothes worn by people in the Bible, what can we learn from this about the metaphorical clothes we dress ourselves in today?

What we wear represents who we are. I'm not talking about our physical garments, but the metaphorical garments that reveal our character and mood. Did you know that your character can wear invisible clothes of unseen colours? Let me explain.

Have you ever been around anyone who is in a *'black mood'* and felt the tension in the room? When someone is sad, we often say they *'look blue'*. Or have you seen the angry person who *'sees red'* because they're so full of rage? We say the jealous person is *'green with envy.'* Or we may have a friend who always seems to be happy like sunshine yellow. Some people are fun-loving and just seem to carry a full set of rainbow colours!

We all subconsciously wear a different colour. The danger comes when we don't pre-decide what we wear. Instead, we allow our ever-changing circumstances to dictate and choose our emotional clothes for us.

But you do know that your emotions can lie to you, right? They can determine the choices we make. They can make us think and believe things are a certain way, coloured by how we're feeling at that particular moment. Not only that, they're often temporary – our emotions can change daily, sometimes hourly!

When we live life on waves of emotion, buffeted by our feelings, we are no different from a child who doesn't know who she wants to be when she grows up. She spends her childhood dressing up, trying on different colours and costumes to see which suits her best. One day she's a princess, the next she's a space cadet!

The wisdom that comes from maturity helps us decide what to wear for what occasion and doesn't depend on our feelings. Maturity knows what is appropriate, comfortable, acceptable and well-fitting in every situation. A confident woman knows who she really is and how to dress, no matter what life throws at her. She understands that just because her circumstances change, she doesn't have to be ruled by her emotions. She pre-decides what to wear and how to act, even if her day isn't going to plan. Who we truly are on the inside doesn't depend on our emotions. We get to decide what we show on the outside. We can clothe ourselves by choice.

I want to remind you today of your heritage, for you are a daughter of the King. That makes you royalty. You too are a woman of noble character, dressed in purple and fine linen, clothes that give you honour and right standing in the presence of a Holy God. You are His child, whatever your circumstances. Your place in His kingdom and company does not change when life is good or when life is at its worst. For our place in God's family is secured, paid for on the cross by Jesus' sacrifice, once and for all.

When you understand who you are and whose you are, you will be able to say with confidence, I am:

- **A daughter of the King**
    "Glorious is the King's daughter within [the palace];
    Her robe is interwoven with gold."
    ~ Psalm 45:13 (AMP: Amplified Bible) ~

- **A God-fearing woman**
    "Charm is deceptive, and beauty is fleeting;
    but a woman who fears the LORD is to be praised."
    ~ Proverbs 31:30 (NIV: New International Version) ~

- **Redeemed**
    "In him we have redemption through his blood,
    the forgiveness of sins, in accordance with the riches of God's grace"
    ~ Ephesians 1:7 (NIV: New International Version) ~

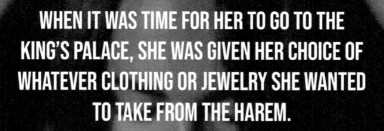

WHEN IT WAS TIME FOR HER TO GO TO THE KING'S PALACE, SHE WAS GIVEN HER CHOICE OF WHATEVER CLOTHING OR JEWELRY SHE WANTED TO TAKE FROM THE HAREM.

ESTHER 2:13 NLT

- **Loved dearly, God paid a high price for me**
  "For I am the LORD your God, the Holy One of Israel, your Savior.
  I give Egypt as your ransom, Cush and Seba in exchange for you."
  ~ Isaiah 43:3 (ESV: English Standard Version) ~

- **Fearfully and wonderfully made**
  "For you formed my inward parts; you knitted me together in my
  mother's womb. I praise you, for I am fearfully and wonderfully made.
  Wonderful are your works; my soul knows it very well."
  ~ Psalm 139:13-14 (ESV: English Standard Version) ~

- **Worth more than rubies**
  "A wife of noble character who can find? She is worth far more than
  rubies."
  ~ Proverbs 31:10 (NIV: New International Version) ~

- **Beautiful beyond make-up and clothes**
  "Your beauty should not come from outward adornment,
  such as elaborate hairstyles and the wearing of gold jewelry or fine clothes.
  Rather, it should be that of your inner self, the unfading beauty of a gentle
  and quiet spirit, which is of great worth in God's sight."
  ~ 1 Peter 3:3-4 (NIV: New International Version) ~

- **Favoured**
  "For those who find me find life and receive favor from the Lord."
  ~ Proverbs 8:35 (NIV: New International Version) ~

- **Strong and Dignified**
  "Then adorn yourself with glory and splendor,
  and clothe yourself in honor and majesty."
  ~ Job 40:10 (NIV: New International Version) ~

- **Fearfully and wonderfully made**
  "She is clothed with strength and dignity,
  and she laughs without fear of the future."
  ~ Proverbs 31:25 (NLT: New Living Translation) ~

- **Transformed**
  "Do not conform to the pattern of this world, but be transformed by the renewing of your mind. Then you will be able to test and approve what God's will is—his good, pleasing and perfect will."
  ~ Romans 12:2 (NIV: New International Version) ~

- **Victorious**
  "I can do all this through him who gives me strength."
  ~ Philippians 4:13 (NIV: New International Version) ~

In the **Book of Esther,** when Queen Esther went to stand before the Persian King Xerxes, the king was not expecting to see her. In fact, anyone who went before the king without a royal invitation was likely to be sentenced to immediate death.

Queen Esther was there to plead for the freedom of her people, the Jewish nation. She was taking a chance, risking her life. But I believe Esther was also smart! She knew that before the king would hear her, he would see her. Therefore, she had to capture his attention with the way she looked before he would hear what she had to say.

"When it was time for her to go to the king's palace, she was given her choice of whatever clothing or jewelry she wanted to take from the harem."
~ Esther 2:13 (NLT: New Living Translation) ~

The Bible doesn't tell us what she chose to wear, but I like to think it was a garment of purple made with fine linen because when she entered the king's quarters, his attention was immediately drawn to her. I think she might have adorned herself in royal colours, indicating her high rank, a prestigious dress befitting for a queen. She would have had the appearance of a woman of virtue, wrapped in dignity and humility and the king would have known *'this woman has right standing to be in my presence. She has my full attention.'*

That day was important in Biblical history because Esther won herself a place in the king's heart and saved her nation.

To every beautiful princess reading this devotional, you will always have God's undivided attention over your life when you purposefully dress to impress the King. Remember, every day you get to choose what you will wear. In the same way that your clothes don't just jump out of the wardrobe and onto your body – you must physically choose them and intentionally put them on – so it is with your mood, your attitude and your spirit.

"So, chosen by God for this new life of love, dress in the wardrobe God picked out for you: compassion, kindness, humility, quiet strength, discipline. Be even-tempered, content with second place, quick to forgive an offense. Forgive as quickly and completely as the Master forgave you. And regardless of what else you put on, wear love. It's your basic, all-purpose garment. Never be without it."
~ Colossians 3:12-14 (MSG: The Message) ~

PRAYER FOR TODAY
Thank you, Jesus, for calling me your daughter and clothing me in royal clothes. May I never throw the overcoat of despair or the jacket of disappointment over my royal robes. May I forever be found dressing my character in a way that is pleasing to you. Amen.

Wear Love.

IT'S YOUR BASIC, ALL-PURPOSE GARMENT. NEVER BE WITHOUT IT.'

COLOSSIANS 3:12-14

DAY TWENTY-SIX
IN THE RIGHT PLACE

"Your body has many parts - limbs, organs, cells - but no matter how many parts you can name, you're still one body. It's exactly the same with Christ."
1 Corinthians 12:12
(MSG: The Message)

HOW TO SPEAK BRAVE

Order is paramount in my home and my family know it. I believe everything has a place. Everyone under my roof knows that if you take your shoes off you need to put them on the shoe rack. If you use the milk, place it back in the fridge when you're done. Dirty dishes go in the dishwasher, not left on the side. Clean dishes have a space and a place in the cupboards. When everything is in its rightful place it helps with the function of our house.

My husband and I have had several disagreements over this in the past. He has a slightly different approach. He goes with the theory, *'things can have many places. Why limit them to one?'* But, let me just say, living like that is chaotic! I repeatedly hear him ask, *"has anyone seen my keys? Do you know where my wallet is? Can you ring my phone, I can't find it!"* And my frustration is this: if they were just put back in their rightful place we wouldn't be playing this game again!

The Apostle Paul, who wrote today's passage of scripture in a letter to the Corinthians, is saying that within the church (the body of Christ) we all have a place. Our specific role, like a different body part, helps the church body to function properly. We may not all have a named leadership position, but we do all have a place. It may not be a place on the stage or platform. It may not be a place of prominence or public recognition. But who you are and where God's placed you is vital for the function of His church.

Did you know that a normal ear has an estimate of between 1000 and 2000 ceruminous glands for producing ear wax? Your eyes contain a sheet of photoreceptors (light-sensitive cells) made up of around 130 million rod cells and 7 million cone cells.

While you were growing in your mother's womb, your brain was growing at a rate of around 250,000 nerve cells per minute, on average, throughout the pregnancy. My point is this: every cell, sinew and fibre in the human body has been strategically placed to enable the body to function to the best of it's ability. If the tongue suddenly decided to be a part of the foot, or if the elbow fancied a position on the forehead, the body would no longer be the body as we know it!

We know from medical science that when something is lacking in the systems of the human body our health takes a hit. Perhaps it's a nutrient deficiency, vitamin or mineral deficiency, or a salt or hormone imbalance. The body takes a hit, strength is reduced, it becomes weak, it gets sick and can't fully function. Though we can't always see it without doing laboratory tests, we know that something is missing which is vital for the proper functioning of the body.

There may be an iron deficiency, meaning we're lacking in red blood cells, or maybe we're losing too much blood. Perhaps there's an iodine deficiency which causes the thyroid to swell. Perhaps there's a deficiency of vitamin D or calcium, causing problems with our bones. All these things, while they may seem small or insignificant, have a huge role to play in our body's function and health.

"In fact, some parts of the body that seem weakest and least important are actually the most necessary. And the parts we regard as less honorable are those we clothe with the greatest care. So we carefully protect those parts that should not be seen, while the more honorable parts do not require this special care. So God has put the body together such that extra honor and care are given to those parts that have less dignity."
1 Corinthians 12:22-24
~ (NLT: New Living Translation) ~

It's often the smallest, most intricate and unassuming parts of our body that we take for granted. We can't see the tiny cells of our inmost organs or our blood vessels, but we know they're there, doing their thing, enabling our body to function so well. You can imagine which body parts Paul might be referring to when he says they seem less presentable or less honourable. We should indeed keep them hidden away when we're out and about in public, but their function is essential never-the-less!

So, in summary beautiful one, I want you to know this: who you are is vital to the life, health and growth of the local church. God has a plan for you and a place for you. When you withdraw, hold back or go missing, the body feels it. The body of Christ needs you to be you, for you have a vital role to play. Similarly, you need to be part of a church to thrive, for the same reason that no limb or body organ can survive detached from its physical body. So you too will begin to die spiritually if you don't have a life source feeding you oxygenated blood – we need to be connected and plugged in.

So remember, in the Father's house there are many rooms. In His house, there is room for you, a place for you, a special function and purpose created just for you. The local church is a home for you to flourish in, Christ's body for you to belong to.

"My Father's house has many rooms; if that were not so, would I have told you that I am going there to prepare a place for you? And if I go and prepare a place for you, I will come back and take you to be with me that you also may be where I am. You know the way to the place where I am going."
John 14:2-4
~ (NIV) New International Version ~

PRAYER FOR TODAY
Lord, help me to find my fit and discover my function within the local church. You didn't create me to be a spare part, but you designed me to be unique, for a purpose within your body, the church. May I do all that I do, not to receive affirmation from other people, but for an audience of one. Lord, I sense your pleasure as I play my part to build your house and establish your Kingdom on earth. Amen.

DAY TWENTY-SEVEN
BEYOND WHAT IS HUMANLY POSSIBLE

"But he said to me, "My grace is sufficient for you, for my power is made perfect in weakness." Therefore I will boast all the more gladly about my weaknesses, so that Christ's power may rest on me."
2 Corinthians 12:9 (NIV: New International Version)

HOW TO REMAIN BRAVE

Have you ever heard the expression, an 'Achilles Heel'?

It is usually a phrase used to describe an area of your life where you feel weakest and most vulnerable, something you feel almost powerless over. It could be a personality flaw, a bad habit, a subconscious downfall, an unconscious pattern you wish you could break but feel you can't, a way of life you have developed that you wish you hadn't, the thing you do that you don't want to do but find yourself doing anyway. Your *weak spot is your Achilles heel*.

Achilles was a hero of Greek Mythology, a man who became a mighty warrior who thought he was invincible. And he almost was, except for that one little vulnerability. His fatal weakness – *his heel*.

According to the mythical legend, Achilles' mother was called Thetis. She was an immortal water goddess. His father was Peleus, who was a mortal king.

Achilles' mother had an obsession with her son's mortality. She was so concerned that she tried different ways to make him immortal, finally taking him to the River Styx, a mythical river that formed the boundary between Earth and the Underworld, the waters of which were believed to be blessed by the gods and whatever the waters touched would never die. She dipped her son into the river and as she did, she kept hold of the back of his foot, consequently his heel never got wet.

Achilles grew to be a mighty warrior but he did have one area of vulnerability. An area of weakness that should the enemy target him in this one area, it would take him down immediately. The legendary tale tells us that Achilles eventually died from an arrow being shot into the back of his heel. Although the story of Achilles is a myth, we still use the phrase Achilles heel today as a metaphor, an expression, a way to describe our weaknesses and fatal flaws. Your Achilles heel might be that thing from your past that you don't want to remember but somehow can't seem to forget. It's the thing you can't get over, the thing you can't move on from, because it's memory is always there.

It could be a mindset that has trapped you, words that were spoken over you, or criticism that has crippled you. Each time you try to move forward in life – to achieve, accomplish, or further yourself – the memory of what was, paralyses you and holds you back. It fills you with fear, dread, shame, and guilt and immediately puts a block on your dreams.

The enemy knows your area of weakness and he will try to get to your Achilles heel in any way that he can. He may use the voice of other people to remind you of what you did, who you were, or where you come from. Sometimes he'll sneak into your thoughts so that your mind is filled with 'what ifs?' 'What if I fail? What if they don't like me? What if it happens again?' This problem is not new to this generation. Throughout history, the enemy has tormented mankind, holding us captive by reminding us of our past mistakes and failures. But God knows how cunning and deceptive the enemy is. He tells us:

"Do not remember the former things, Or ponder the things of the past. Listen carefully, I am about to do a new thing, Now it will spring forth; Will you not be aware of it? I will even put a road in the wilderness, Rivers in the desert."
~ Isaiah 43:18-19 (AMP: Amplified Bible) ~

Do not remember the former things! That means don't reflect, don't rehearse, don't ruminate or dwell on the past. Choose not to remember!

God knows you are exhausted, living life on the merry-go-round of torment. He's aware of what the enemy has stolen from you, how he's bound up your hopes, seized your mind and held captive your confidence.

He walked into your life when you were at your most vulnerable, stole your identity, twisted your morals, took your innocence, took your dignity and fed you a diet of lies and shame. I believe God wants to awaken you to who you truly are. Although you've made mistakes in the past, your mistakes are not who you are. Firstly, you are His daughter and you carry his resemblance.

"So God created human beings in his own image. In the image of God he created them, male and female he created them."
~ Genesis 1:27 (NLT: New Living Translation) ~

Secondly, God made it very clear to satan that though you torment her, when she releases the authority she possesses as my daughter, she will crush you!

"And I will put enmity between you and the woman, and between your offspring and hers; he (she) will crush your head, and you will strike his (her) heel."
~ Genesis 3:15 (NIV: New International Version) ~

I really wish God had enmity between the serpent and the man, but he didn't. The enmity, the war, was set out between the woman and the serpent. Satan, your greatest enemy will always be after your heel, the weakest and most vulnerable part of your life, but God wants to remind you today that **your bruised heel can still crush his head today!**

So, every time the enemy wants to bring you down or make you feel small by reminding you of your past, you can remind him of your future!

- **God empowers me**
  "I can do all things through Christ who strengthens me."
  ~ Philippians 4:13 (NKJV: New King James Version) ~

- **God says I am His**
  "Fear not, for I have redeemed you;
  I have called you by your name; You are Mine."
  ~ Isaiah 43:1 (NKJV: New King James Version) ~

- **God says I am made new**
  "Therefore, if anyone is in Christ, the new creation has come:
  The old has gone, the new is here!"
  ~ 2 Corinthians 5:17 (NIV: New International Version) ~

- **God says I am accepted**
  "So Peter opened his mouth and said: "Truly I understand that God shows
  no partiality, but in every nation anyone who fears him
  and does what is right is acceptable to him."
  ~ Acts 10:34-35 (ESV: English Standard Version) ~

- **God says I am the apple of His eye**
  "For this is what the Lord Almighty says: "After the Glorious One has
  sent me against the nations that have plundered you—
  for whoever touches you touches the apple of his eye"
  ~ Zechariah 2:8 (NIV: New International Version) ~

- **God says He has a plan for my life**
  "For I know the plans I have for you," declares the Lord, "plans to
  prosper you and not to harm you, plans to give you hope and a future."
  ~ Jeremiah 29:11 (NIV: New International Version) ~

- **God says I am forgiven**
  "Praise the Lord, my soul, and forget not all his benefits—
  who forgives all your sins and heals all your diseases..."
  ~ Psalm 103:2-3 (NIV: New International Version) ~

- **God says I am created for a purpose**
  "For we are God's handiwork, created in Christ Jesus to do good works,
  which God prepared in advance for us to do."
  ~ Ephesians 2:10 (NIV: New International Version) ~

PRAYER FOR TODAY

Father God, I am your child, created in your image. I know who I am, I know whose I am. I do not have to doubt your love for me because of my past failures or worry about what the future holds for me. The declarations written in your word are powerful and you have equipped me with everything I need to silence the enemy and strengthen the 'inner me'. I am not identified by my mistakes. I am a daughter of the King, mighty like a warrior, brave as can be, and everywhere I go, I know my God is with me. Amen.

MY GRACE IS **SUFFICIENT** FOR YOU, FOR MY POWER IS MADE PERFECT IN WEAKNESS. THEREFORE I WILL BOAST ALL THE MORE GLADLY ABOUT MY WEAKNESSES, SO THAT **CHRIST'S POWER** MAY REST ON ME

2 CORINTHIANS 12:9

DAY TWENTY-EIGHT
LIVING A BLESSED LIFE

> *"Blessed is the one who does not walk in step with the wicked or stand in the way that sinners take or sit in the company of mockers, but whose delight is in the law of the Lord, and who meditates on his law day and night. That person is like a tree planted by streams of water, which yields its fruit in season and whose leaf does not wither — whatever they do prospers."*
> *Psalm 1:1-3*
> *(NIV: New International Version)*

HOW TO REMAIN BRAVE

The earliest memories I have of my nan are of her dancing around the kitchen in her pinny (she was always baking), singing at the top of her voice:

"I am blessed, I am blessed
I am blessed. When I wake up in the morning, till I lay my head to rest,
I am blessed, I am blessed,
I am blessed."

She would dance across the kitchen, whirling her rolling pin around like a conductor's baton, as she anthemically sang these words.

As a child, I had no idea or understanding of what she was singing about. But now as an adult, I reflect on her life and realise that the blessing she sang of was not an academic achievement (she was poorly educated, left school aged 9 and entered a workhouse). The blessing wasn't to do with material possessions (she seriously had nothing worth shouting about). Yet she would loudly and openly confess *"I am blessed, I am blessed, I am blessed!"* because she understood that blessings are not based on circumstances but rather based on the character of God.

She was expressing her gratitude for the goodness, kindness, generosity and faithfulness that God had shown towards her throughout her lifetime.

My lovely nan became pregnant out of wedlock aged 16 years old in the late 1930s. This was in the days when this was socially stigmatised. She was ostracised (excluded), criticised and cast aside (rejected) by many including her own family. She was even shunned by the church. She lived in the heart of Liverpool during World War II and survived the Blitz, including a bomb crashing through the roof of her house (but miraculously, it got caught in the beams and rafters, hovering unexploded, suspended above her bed).

She raised five daughters, one of whom had special needs. In the post-war era, there was very little social support and not much understanding of how to help care for such children and their development. She battled cancer and won!

She lived a very frugal life and certainly didn't have much in the way of possessions. And yet she considered herself a very blessed woman! What my nan did have was a love for God and a passion for His Word and she understood the importance of living out the scriptures she would read.

She knew that a blessed life didn't mean a problem-free life but rather it was a *'look how I've come through'* life.

We cannot pick and choose which difficulties we will encounter during our lifetime, but we can determine how we will go through them. How you go through the challenges and trials of life will determine how you come out on the other side – *depressed or blessed!*

The Book of Psalms reads like a songbook or poetry book, many of them were written by David. **Psalm 1** is one of the anonymous Psalms, which we believe may have been written by David, but could have possibly been written by his son, Solomon.

In this Psalm he gives us some keys to living a blessed life (a life with Gods favour on it).

David knew only too well that life can throw you curve balls, things you don't see coming. Throughout your life, you may drop a few balls too and make some mistakes. We all have regrets of some form or another.

King David messed his life up *big time*. Lies were told, adultery was committed, he even covered up a murder, lost a child, was rejected by friends and found himself on the run more than once. He embarrassed himself and embarrassed God, won some battles, lost some battles. There were times when he knew what it was to be an outcast and that some friendships don't last and yet in reflection of his life he writes Psalm 1 telling us he is a blessed man. He wrote:

1. Do not walk in step with the wicked

'Blessed is the one…who does not…walk in the steps of the wicked'

If you are walking in step with someone, you are walking in unity, agreeing to their ways and to their behaviour. If you are walking in step with someone, you are intentionally going in the same direction with them. You will ultimately reach the same destination.

When the Bible refers to 'the wicked' in this context, it is referring to those who do not have the same Christian values, morals or belief system as you. Their steps will take you away from God and His plan for your life.

So be careful who you partner up with and who you forge relationships with. Whether it's in the dating season, in marriage, or in business, who you align yourself with will take you in a certain direction. So be sure you know where you want your life to be headed before you agree to walk with someone.

2. Do not stand in the way of sinners.

'Blessed is the one…who does not…stand in the way of sinners'

A stand is a stance, this scripture is saying **'blessed is the one who does not stand in the same way as sinners.'** Our stance, position and posture can speak volumes without us having to say a word.

When someone stands with folded arms or hands on their hips, whether they are standing tall or slouching, our posture reveals our attitude. We have an inner posture that the human eye can't see, but God sees us clearly, for He sees our hearts. Have you ever thought about what your inner posture looks like? I think the author is saying here, be careful who you associate with, because who they are can rub off on you.

Don't say 'yes' with your mouth but have a 'no' in your heart. Don't smile on the outside and be filled with hate on the inside. Jealousy, pride, unforgiveness, all these things are the stance of a sinner.

Your life will be blessed when your posture is right.

3. Do not take a seat in the company of mockers

'Blessed is the one...who does not...take a seat in the company of mockers'

To 'take a seat' means to get comfortable, to linger, to hang out with someone and keep them company. A 'mocker' is someone with a critical spirit, who scoffs and looks down on others, putting other people down to make themselves feel better. Anytime you listen to the gossip or engage in conversation with someone who is a gossiper, or a sower of discord and division, then you have just pulled up a seat in the company of a mocker.

Sometimes the bravest thing you can do is to go against the world's version of normal and that looks like NOT doing these three things above but DOING this one thing...

4. Meditate on God's law, day and night

'Blessed is the one...who meditates on God's law, day and night'

That simply means to have an awareness 24/7 that God is with you. He is the silent listener to every conversation. The ever present father. Think about Him being present in every area and circumstance of your life. Ask yourself, *'what would God want me to say in this situation? How should I respond? How should I pray?'*

Allowing God to be a part of your daily life should be as easy as drawing breath. You don't have to think about it, yet it's the very thing that keeps you alive.

> *"That person is like a tree planted by streams of water,*
> *which yields its fruit in season and whose leaf does not wither—*
> *whatever they do prospers."*
> *~ Psalm 1:3 (NIV: New International Version) ~*

God can cause your life to prosper despite the mistakes you have made, the heartache you have endured, and the misfortunes that have occurred.

When you live your life, adhering to these three 'do not's' and in obedience to this one 'do', God will always come through for you and you too can burst into song declaring 'I am blessed, I am blessed, I am blessed!'

PRAYER FOR TODAY
Father, I thank you that you have given us these instructions on how to live a blessed life. Give me the strength and the courage to do what is right in your sight and not conform to the normal patterns of this world. I want to live under the blessings of Heaven. I ask this in Jesus' name. Amen.

DAY TWENTY-NINE
BEAUTY FROM WITHIN

"Charm can be misleading, and beauty is vain and so quickly fades, but this virtuous woman lives in the wonder, awe, and fear of the Lord. She will be praised throughout eternity. So go ahead and give her the credit that is due, for she has become a radiant woman, and all her loving works of righteousness deserve to be admired at the gateways of every city!"
Proverbs 31:30-31
(TPT: The Passion Translation)

HOW TO REMAIN BRAVE

Did you know that no matter how often we get our nails manicured, our hair coloured, our lashes done and make-up on, we cannot stop the effects of ageing? The truth is that external beauty does have an expiry date.

There is however, a type of beauty that never grows old. In fact, this type becomes more beautiful over time and radiates as we age, a beauty so unique that it turns the heads of all who encounter it. It captivates Heaven and attracts God's attention. It may not seem pretty on the outside, nor attractive to the human eye. That's because this type of beauty reveals itself on the inside. It looks like the dignified strength and resilience that comes from a heart broken by disappointment and pain, yet refuses to stop believing in the faithfulness of God's name.

Let me show you what this kind of beauty looks like through the life of a woman called Hannah. Her story is told in **1 Samuel 1**.

Hannah prayed for many years to have a baby. The Bible describes her deep anguish, meaning; severe suffering or distress.

Year after year, month after month she remained childless. Yet despite her disappointment and heartache, she never gave up hope, believing that God could do a miracle through her barren womb.

Now, if you've got a mental image of Hannah praying sweetly as a serene woman on bended knee with her hands together and her eyes closed, think again! Rather, imagine her with black mascara streaming down her cheeks, snot flying, tears flowing, and wailing – and you've almost got the picture!

Hannah wasn't just praying to God. She was broken and sobbing before Him, weeping bitterly. She was such a mess that Eli, the temple priest, even thought she was drunk!

"As she kept on praying to the Lord, Eli observed her mouth. Hannah was praying in her heart, and her lips were moving but her voice was not heard. Eli thought she was drunk and said to her, "How long are you going to stay drunk? Put away your wine."
~ 1 Samuel 1:12-14 (NIV: New International Version) ~

I don't know if you know what it is to be broken before God. But when you've hit the point of desperation in such a way that your entire body aches for a breakthrough, your heart longs for a miracle or even just a glimmer of hope, well this is how we find Hannah.

Eli the priest was sat in the gateway of the temple where Hannah was praying and I'm not sure exactly what he observed. Perhaps it was Hannah's body language, perhaps in her deep anguish she seemed uncoordinated in her movements, out of control with her emotions, unable to stand. Anyway, he thought she looked drunk. But she was far from it. She was simply heartbroken and devastated, pouring out her pain to God, as she made this promise:

"O LORD of Heaven's Armies, if you will look upon my sorrow and answer my prayer and give me a son, then I will give him back to you. He will be yours for his entire lifetime, and as a sign that he has been dedicated to the LORD his hair will never be cut."
~ 1 Samuel 1:11 (NLT: New Living Translation) ~

Let me just say, prayers like that are still getting answered today!

I wonder sometimes if God allows our dreams to be delayed to reveal more of what is really in our hearts. The longer Hannah waited, the more her heart ached, and a beautiful spirit was revealed within her. It wasn't a beauty that anyone could see on the outside, for her outer appearance was a mess, but her inner beauty was magnetic to God. It was a sacrificial prayer, *'I lay down all of me before all that You are'.* I think of the many things that we ask God for, the promises and bargains we so easily make:

* *Lord, if only I could get married to a Godly man, we would both serve You.'*
* *Lord, if you could just give me a pay rise, then I would give You more.'*
* *Lord, if you could just give me the dream house, then I would open it up and invite Your people in.'*

Only, when that time eventually does come for your prayer to be answered, it's so easy to focus on the gift and forget the gift-giver. We can get so caught up serving the vision (of your career, your home, or your soft furnishings), that God and the promise we made to Him are very easily forgotten. How easy it is to bargain with God, *'Lord, if only I could have a baby, I would raise my child in Your house and forever declare Your goodness.'* Well, as soon as the baby arrives things get very busy very quickly. It's hard to find enough hours in the week and get to church as well, what with everything else there is to do. And so your promise may get forgotten and the House of God takes a back seat to all your other priorities.

But Hannah remained true to her word and in return, the Lord blessed her with a son. When her long-awaited son, Samuel, was weaned (around 5 years old, Bible Scholars think) she took him back to the very temple where she had first prayed and handed him over to Eli the priest to be trained and raised to become a man of God. But the true miracle is found in what happened next:

> *"But Samuel was ministering before the Lord—a boy wearing a linen ephod. Each year his mother made him a little robe and took it to him when she went up with her husband to offer the annual sacrifice. Eli would bless Elkanah and his wife, saying, "May the Lord give you children by this woman to take the place of the one she prayed for and gave to the Lord." Then they would go home. And the Lord was gracious to Hannah; she gave birth to three sons and two daughters. Meanwhile, the boy Samuel grew up in the presence of the Lord."*
> *~ 1 Samuel 2:18-21 (NIV: New International Version) ~*

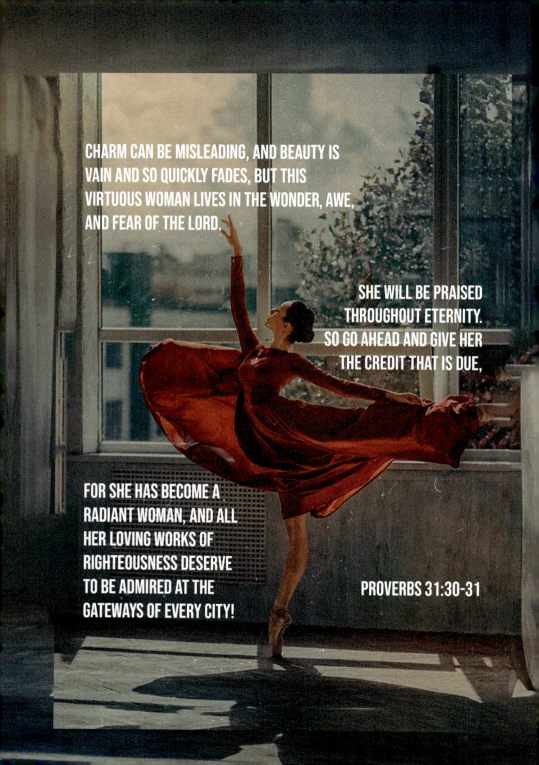

Because Hannah had honoured her promise to God by giving Him her first-born son, God blessed her, by opening her womb and she went on to have a further five children.

"Give, and it will be given to you. A good measure, pressed down, shaken together and running over, will be poured into your lap. For with the measure you use, it will be measured to you."
~ Luke 6:38 (NIV: New International Version) ~

God can multiply the little we have and return it to us. Ordinarily, we want to hold on to what we have. But it's a brave thing to entrust your little to God, surrendering our all to Him. *'Give, and it will be given to you.'*

When Hannah prayed that prayer, she was only believing for one child. But here's the thing, whatever you place in the hands of God only ever increases. Your marriage gets better, your finances increase, your health improves, and your life begins to flourish. That's what true beauty looks like: total surrender to God, never quitting, always hoping, keeping on believing that *'my God will meet all your needs according to the riches of his glory in Christ Jesus.'*

Remaining brave looks like trusting God, even in the most difficult of seasons.

"...this virtuous woman lives in the wonder, awe, and fear of the Lord. She will be praised throughout eternity."
~ Proverbs 31:30 (TPT: The Passion Translation) ~

PRAYER FOR TODAY
Lord, may I always trust you, your ways and your timing. You know what I need most and when I should have it. You're never a minute too early or a moment too late. You answer me on time, every time. But in my waiting season, dear Lord, may I press into you with my everything and may you find my heart to be in total pursuit of you. Increase my beauty before your eyes, O Lord, as I hold on to hope in the expectation of what you are going to do. Amen.

DAY THIRTY
A SAFE JOURNEY

> *"There is a way that appears to be right, but in the end it leads to death."*
> *Proverbs 14:12 (NIV: New International Version)*

WISDOM'S CALL

"Does not wisdom call out?
Does not understanding raise her voice?
At the highest point along the way,
where the paths meet, she takes her stand"
~ *Proverbs 8:1-2 (NIV: New International Version)* ~

HOW TO REMAIN BRAVE

Road traffic accidents can happen for several reasons including carelessness, dangerous driving and bad habits. We know that many incidents occur because a driver has deviated from the '*The Highway Code.*'

Maybe the driver thought it would be okay to skip through the lights as they changed from amber to red. Perhaps they presumed it wouldn't be a problem to drive faster than the speed limit. Or maybe they ignored the signs warning them of a junction up ahead.

The Highway Code is not just a rule book, telling us what we can and can't do whilst driving on our roads. Neither is it just a book of suggestions, open to interpretation. Rather, it is a book of clear instructions, that should you adhere to them, you will drive safely, you will get to your destination and you will lessen the risk of endangering yourself or others along the way.

The reason you take a driving test is to prove to the DVLA that you have studied and understood the Highway Code.

Life works in a similar way. The Bible, and all it contains, is a bit like an instruction manual. In particular, the Book of Proverbs is filled with instructions and advice that, should we choose to follow it, will lead us to a life where we succeed, flourish and win. During our lifetime we will all encounter our fair share of difficulties. We will experience problems and pain, heartache, struggles and strain. No one is exempt. But here's the really great thing: You do not have to navigate those difficult times alone. You don't have to guess your way through.

The Bible is our spiritual highway code. It will teach you to spot the warning signs, how to overcome the obstacles you face. It will show you how to remain steadfast when you feel like giving up and forwarn you when there is change on the horizon of your life.

The Bible is not irrelevant, ancient and boring. The words contained within it are life-giving if we adhere to them.

Could you imagine what driving along our roads would be like if the Highway Code did not exist? If there were no road signs and nobody followed the rules, it would be carnage!

I believe there are spiritual road signs throughout the scriptures that are there to show us what is ahead on our journey through life. Scriptures like our text today encourage us not to choose a certain way just because it feels right:

"There is a way that appears to be right, but in the end it leads to death."
~ Proverbs 14:12 (NIV) New International Version ~

When we find ourselves at a crossroads in life, when we are faced with a difficult decision to make, we need to be mindful that just because something feels right, that doesn't mean it is right.

Ultimately, we were all fated to choose the way to death until we were saved by Jesus, who restored us to eternal life.

The word '*death*' in our scripture today does not mean literal death, it means death as in – '*nothing good will come from this,*' '*nothing healthy will grow from it.*' A dumb decision is a dead-end decision, and you can apply that to so many different areas of life, like when you're looking for a partner, physical attraction is important but it cannot be the sole reason for commitment. If his beliefs are not aligned with yours, if his morals differ from yours, if he values different things to you - although everything feels good right now, the relationship will eventually die. Though the job may feel right and you have said yes to the contract because it looked good on paper and you got excited in the moment, if you didn't first ask the Lord to direct your steps then it just may lead to a dead-end.

"Trust in the Lord with all of your heart and do not lean on your own understanding, in all of your ways acknowledge him and he will make straight your paths."
~ Proverbs 3:5-6 (ESV: English Standard Version) ~

We need to trust the Lord with all of our heart. We can't rely on our feelings and our own limited understanding.

Pray and seek the Lord, ask Him to direct you in your decision-making and familiarise yourself with His word (your spiritual highway code). Be aware of any '*Road Narrows*' signs that may be indicating that this part of your journey is for single-lane traffic only. To take the narrow road, God might be asking you to let go of some friendships *because you need to choose* a different route.

After all, Jesus said in the Book of Matthew:

"Enter through the narrow gate. For wide is the gate and broad is the road that leads to destruction, and many enter through it. But small is the gate and narrow the road that leads to life, and only a few find it."
~ Matthew 7:13-14 (NIV: New International Version) ~

It may look like:

- Saying no to the party – because you know what's going on there isn't good for you.
- Not entertaining idle chit-chat that you know will turn into gossip.
- Not cutting corners in your business as you'll lose your integrity.
- Walking away from so-called friends who bring out the worst in you.

These are all '*road narrowing*' moments and we need to have the wisdom to not just follow the crowd. Just because it feels good, just because everyone else seems to be doing it, doesn't mean we have to go that way too. So choose your route wisely, by putting God, His Word and His ways first.

There may be a road sign indicating that there's a roundabout up ahead. If you're not clear on the direction your life is going, if you don't have a destination in mind, and you're just drifting along instead of being intentional, you could find yourself stuck going around in circles for a long time.

So, before you date the guy, before you start the business, before you spend the money, before you get on the roundabout of decision, first choose where you're headed. Know your end goal. Remind yourself who you are and whose you are, so that when someone tries to take your life in a direction that is contrary to the one God has promised to you, you will have the clarity and the wisdom to say, "This is a wrong direction for me. I'm going a different way."

PRAYER FOR TODAY
God, help me to always seek you first for wisdom and direction. May I not guess my way through life, especially in the life-defining moments of decision-making. I trust in the power of your word, and I thank you that you have given me spiritual road signs to guide me and keep me on the right pathway. Amen.

ABOUT THE AUTHOR

Emma Bryant

Emma is a pastor and speaker who has a contagious passion for God and a desire to help set others up strong, to live out their best lives through the teachings and principles from His Word.

Emma is the founder of Braveheart, a fast-growing women's movement that has reached and touched many, many girls from all walks of life.

She truly believes that the relationship you have with yourself sets the tone for every other relationship you will ever have, therefore, it is important to take time out to invest into you.

Emma's practical application to communicating God's word makes it fun to learn and relevant to life.

Alongside her husband Luke, they are the founders and lead pastors of Liverpool One Church in the heart of the city of Liverpool. Emma and Luke are passionate about people falling in love with God and finding a home in the local church. They have three sons, Joash, Isaac and Solomon, one daughter-in-love Jessie and a handsome little G-baby, Ezra.

146